THE PRODUCERS

A DESCRIPTIVE DIRECTORY OF FILM AND TELEVISION PRODUCERS IN THE LOS ANGELES AREA

COMPILED AND EDITED BY RICHARD BURGER

Graphic Design by Christine Soldenski.
Thanks to her also for proofreading and pasteup.

ISBN 0-914561-03-0

You may order copies of this directory prepaid directly from the publisher at $8 per copy. Make checks payable to: Richard Burger.

And send to: THE PRODUCERS
             Dept B
             PO Box 1016
             Venice, CA 90294-1016

© MCMLXXXV by Richard Burger

INTRODUCTION TO FOURTH EDITION

This fourth edition is 25% larger than the third.

Two hundred companies have been added.

In terms of total personnel, THE PRODUCERS, fourth edition, has the names and positions of over 2000 personnel of the nearly 1000 companies listed.

An Index has been added in the back. This Index is over 15 pages in length and makes the book much more valuable as a daily reference book of Los Angeles' film/TV industry.

Each listing has been checked for accuracy and updated. Essentially the information in the listings is how the producers see themselves; and we cannot guarantee that you will find each company to be exactly as it sees itself.

The directory contains the producers of features, TV movies, TV mini-series, TV series, TV specials, commercials, cable TV, Pay TV, business and industrial films, educational films, religious programming, documentaries, sports films, health films, and music videotapes. The listing contains TV stations, cable systems, animators.

The directory also contains about 75 listings of companies that are not really producers yet whose names are frequently found on lists of producers: these are companies with businesses essential to the film/videotape industry: e.g. editors, sound technicians, and so on.

The many improvements in this fourth edition are the result of your comments - by letter and phone. Future editions will continue to be corrected, improved, and enlarged as you let me know how you use the book and what you would like added.

USING THIS DIRECTORY

Name

The directory is in alphabetical order. When a person's first and last name form part of the company title, the lising is according to the last name - unless the producer requested otherwise.

Terminology

F/V

Each description begins with an abbreviation, indicative of the medium (or media) in which the producer works. F=film; V=videtotape; M=multimedia; FS=filmstrip; S=slides. If more than one medium is listed then the first listed is that in which the producer does the more work.

Features

This term is used for all feature length motion pictures whether produced for the theatre or television.

Shorts

This term describes a film or videotape product whose length is less than that of a feature; and which is generally made for speciifc markets: business & industry (B&I in this directory), education, medicine, religion, etc.

Animation

Indicates that the company has both the personnel and the equipment for the production of animation whether cel or computer.

(YEAR/#)

Each listing concludes with a number within paren-
thesis. The first number is the year the company
was founded. The number following the slashmark is
the number of persons employed full time by the
producer.

Abbreviations

Other abbreviations used within the directory should
be self explanatory:

E.G.

assoc. prod.	= associate producer
CEO	= chief executive officer
COO	= chief operating officer
dir.	= director
exec. prod.	= executive producer
prod.	= producer
vp	= vice president
sen vp	= senior vice president
pres.	= president

A

A & A Productions   (213) 462-2632
1438 N. Gower #19, Hollywood 90028
F: commercials, cable TV including Long Beach Grand
Prix Pro-Celebrity Race.

A & M Films   (213) 469-2411
1416 N. La Brea Ave, Hollywod 90028
F: features. Gil Friesen, president; Andy Meyer,
exec vp. Subsidiary of A & M Records. (1981/3)

Abby Lou Entertainment   (818) 506-8199
3855 Lankershim Blvd, Universal City 91604
F/V: children's programing. George LeFave. (1974/5)

ABC   (213) 557-7777
2040 Avenue of the Stars, Los Angeles 90067
Studio: 4151 Prospect Ave., Los Angeles 90027
American Broadcasting Company, Incorporated:
Frederick S. Pierce, president. ABC Broadcast Group:
Tony Thomopoulos, president. Incorporated divisions:

ABC Motion Pictures (features): Brandon Stoddard,
president; Herb Jellinek, vp-production. Christy L.
Welker, vp novels and limited series for TV. Bruce
Sallan, vp motion pictures for TV.
Theatrical division: Rene Missel, vp West Coast
production.

ABC Television Network: James Duffy, president; ABC
Entertainment: Lewis H. Erlicht, president. Develop-
ment personnel: Ann Daniel, vp prime time series;
Stu Bloomberg, vp comedy, Jordan Kerner, vp drama.

Other divisions: ABC Pictures International (foreign
distribution); ABC Wide World of Learning (school
and library distribution); ABC Video Sales (retail-
ing of properties).

Aberdeen Video (213) 874-3050
3349 Cahuenga Blvd West #1A, Los Angeles 90068
Videotape editing: 3/4". Russ Levine, owner.

Robert Able & Associates (213) 462-8100
953 N. Highland, Los Angeles 90038
F: commercials.

Academy Productions (818) 985-5988
10000 Riverside Dr #18, Toluca Lake 91602
F/V: features, documentaries, commercials.

The Act Factory (213) 851-1400
1314 N. Hayworth Ave. Suite 402, Los Angeles 90046
M: B&I, including live theatre and entertainment.
Provides acts for performing artists, and perform-
ance workshops. A division of Myriad Productions. Ed
Harris, pres-exec prod. (1965)

Acton Cable TV (714) 946-6607
1208 W. 9th St, Upland 91786
Multiple cable systems with other offices in Glendora & Rialto. Kerry Jurgens, local origination
coordinator.

Adams & Adams Films (818) 360-4556
17233 Warrrington Dr, Granada Hills 91344
F/V: documentaries, TV series, & pilots. Office in
Austin. (1974/2)

Adventist Media Productions (805) 498-4561
1100 Rancho Conejo Blvd, Newbury Park 91320
F/V: specialty is religious materials but also produces material more broadly in the educational
field. Colin Nead, production desginer; Jerry Reed,
film & video services. (1974/4)

Advisual Productions (714) 552-1645
17262 Candleberry, Irvine 92715
F: public relations films for business.

African Family Films (213) 392-1020
P O Box 1109, Venice 90291
F: documentaries, fiction: West and East Africa. Jim
Rosellini, pres; Ron Mulvihill, associate. (1975)

Afton Productions　　　　(213) 466-9351
6245 Afton Place, Hollywood 90028
See: Pavillion Communications.

Aims Media　　　　(818) 785-4111
6901 Woodley Ave, Van Nuys 91406-4878
F: B&I, education, health films; also law enforcement training films. Sales and rental library. Juanell Brackin, office manager.

Airline Film & TV Promotions　　　　(818) 899-1151
13246 Weidner St, Pacoima 91331
Rents theatrical mockups of passenger airplanes and airport sets; provides airport locations. 35mm stock footage of airplane-related material. Byron Schmidt, pres; Alf Jacobsen vp.

The Aldan Company　　　　(213) 936-1082
355 S. Mansfield Ave, Los Angeles 90036
F: features, including Night of the Demon, Adonis Factor. Jim Ball, PhD, pres. (1963/15)

The Aldrich Company　　　　(213) 462-6511
606 North Larchmont Suite 209, Los Angeles 90004
F: Robert Aldrich, prod-dir. of features, including All the Marbles. (1954)

All West Video　　　　(818) 508-8500
11320 Chandler Blvd, N. Hollywood 91601
Post production 3/4" videotape facility. Don Buccola, vp.

Irwin Allen Productions　　　　(818) 954-3601
Columbia Plaza, Burbank 91505
F:features and television series.

Allend'or Productions Inc　　　　(818) 986-4622
15036 Valley Vista Blvd,
Preferred: P O Box 5550, Sherman Oaks 91403
F: educational & B&I. (1953/3)

The Alpha Corporation
726 Upham, San Luis Obispo CA 93401
F: features.

Alphyco Productions   **(213) 469-8363**
6525 Sunset Blvd #A, Hollywood 90028
Television, theatre, and film production. Producers:
A. Christopher Hoffman, Bobby Jacoby.

Alta Marea Productions Inc   **(818) 842-2135**
3808 Riverside Dr, Burbank 91505
Markets and licenses products shown on TV or movies;
also motion picture promotion (press/videotape/film)
& props and sportswear placement. (1977/11)

AM Productions   **(818) 449-0683**
46 S. DeLacey Ave, Pasadena 91105
F/V/M: B&I. Art Michaud, gen manager. (1975/3)

American Biograph Company, Inc   **(213) 274-5316**
9025 Wilshire Blvd #206, Beverly Hills 90211
F/V: TV series, commercials, B&I, features. Broadway
production. Mitchell Jayson, exec prod; Peter R.J.
Deyell prod/dir. Founded by D.W. Griffith. (1908/78

American Cablevision of Orange   **(714) 997-6678**
333 N. Glassell St, Orange 92666
Cable franchise with local origination channel. Jay
Libby, director of community programing.

American Eagle Productions   **(213) 321-1798**
340 W. 131st St, Los Angeles 90061
Not a production company. Theme parties.

American Flyer   **(213) 208-1441**
10201 W. Pico Blvd, Los Angeles CA 90035
F: features and TV series including The Yellow Rose.

American Pacific Video Inc (AMPAC)   **(213) 851-7200**
3637 Cahuenga Blvd West, Los Angeles 90068
Videotape editing: 3/4". Sharman West.

Amicus Productions, Inc   **(213) 874-3073**
1012 N. Sycamore, Los Angeles 90038
F/V/M: B&I. Jerry Rosenbloom, pres. (1973/6)

Amoya Productions   **(805) 654-1575**
P O Box 390, Los Angeles 90028
F/V: commercials, TV specials. Bill Moya, pres.
(1979/13)

4

Robert Amram Films   **(213) 852-1462**
8741 Shoreham Dr, Los Angeles 90069
F: documentaries.

Anacapa Productions   **(213) 654-8328**
7632 Lexington Ave, Los Angeles 90046
F/V: Film and TV production. Harison Ingels, pres.
(1979/3)

J.E. Andary Theatrical Product. & Fin.(213) 466-3379
7080 Hollywood Blvd #114, Los Angeles 90028
F/V: all types production. And distribution. (1948)

Howard A Anderson Company   **(213) 463-2336**
1016 N. Cole Ave, Hollywood 90038
F/V: special photographic effects. Aerial image
optical printers; production insert facilities;
titles, matte, optical, trick effects. (1927/30)

Tom Anderson Filmworks   **(213) 464-0386**
6362 Hollywood Blvd, #308, Hollywood 90028
F: titles, special effects. Stock footage. (1972/5)

Animation Filmakers Corp (AFC)   **(213) 277-5295**
7000 Romaine St, Hollywood 90038
F: cel animation. TV series, B&I, educational films.
Richard Brown, producer; Eric Norquist, production
manager.

Anson Productions Inc   **(213) 201-7163**
1888 Century Pk East-5th Fl, Los Angeles 90067
F: features (including Skyward), TV series (Little-
shots), and documentaries. Barbara Hiser, development. (1976)

Apogee, Inc   **(818) 989-5757**
6842 Valjean Ave, Van Nuys 91406
F: special effects for features. John Dysktra.
(1978)

Apple Productions Inc   **(213) 462-0995**
6240 Afton Place, Hollywood 90028
F/V: B&I, education, cable TV. Jeff Apple, producer-
dir. (1976/30)

Apple/Rose Productions　　　　　　　　(213) 462-0995
6240 Afton Place, Hollywood 90028
F: feature development and production. Jeff Apple,
producer; Robert Rosenthal, writer-dir.

Appledown Films　　　　　　　　　(213) 552-0577
2029 Century Park East, Los Angeles 90067
See: Spiegel-Bergman Productions.

Argus Productions, Inc　　　　　　(213) 274-2891
15212 La Maida St, Sherman Oaks 91403
F: features. F.A. Nicholson, pres. (1975)

Armstrong Creative Services, Ltd　(818) 506-7227
11846 Ventura Blvd 2nd fl, Studio City 91604
F: commercials, promotions, TV specials. (1974/4)

Samuel Z. Arkoff Co　　　　　　　(213) 278-7600
9200 Sunset Blvd, Penthouse 3, Los Angeles 90069
F/V: features, including Rafts. Samuel Arkoff, president; Louis Arkoff, vp.

Arista Films Inc　　　　　　　　(818) 907-7660
16027 Ventura Blvd. #305, Encino 91436
F: features. Foreign distribution. Louis George,
pres; Lawrence G. Garrett, sales & acquisitions.
(1974/5).

Arteffex　　　　　　　　　　　(818) 701-5994
19830 Merridy St, Chatsworth 91311
F/V: features; music video, special effects. Richard
Schmit, exec prod. (1977/3)

Artemis Productions, Ltd　　　　(213) 876-9575
PO Box 691501, Los Angeles 90069
Motion picture production company. Diane Baker,
producer.

Artist Consultants Productions, Inc　(213) 273-5050
11777 San Vicente Blvd, Los Angeles 90049

Ashton-Kochmann Productions　　(213) 653-6870
309 S. Orlando Ave, Los Angeles 90048
V: TV specials for cable. Also live night club
revues. Wolf Kochmann, pres; Barry Ashton, sec-
treasurer. (1961/6)

Aspect Ratio, Inc (213) 467-2121
1514 Crossroads of the World, Hollywood 90028
Feature promotions, TV & radio commercials. Robert
Israel; Ron Moler. (1978/6)

Asselin Productions (213) 653-6190
8489 West Third St, Los Angeles 90048
F/V: TV specials for children (including Zertigo
Diamond Caper); cable. Janet Fisher Buckley, production supervisor. (1976/4)

Associated Communications (213) 457-7611
32554 Pacific Coast Hwy, Malibu 90265
F: features. A subsidiary of Assoc. Commun. Corp,
Ltd, of which Lord Lew Grade is CEO.

Associated Film Enterprises (213) 273-5844
P O Box 2879, Beverly Hills 90213
F: features. Steve Broidy.

Associated TV International (213) 858-7842
PO Box 4180, Hollywood 90078
TV and motion picture production for syndication &
network TV; also syndication. Trevor Batkin, pres.;
Paul Sharratt, vp.

Associates & Toback (213) 464-2157
6532 Sunset Blvd, Hollywood 90028
F: commercials. (1971/7)

Astrofilm Service (213) 851-1673
932 N. La Brea Ave, Hollywood 90038
Film negative cutting. David Pappmeier, pres. (1967)

Jack Atlas Organization (213) 476-7176
P O Box 241428, Los Angeles CA 90024
Consultation: production, publicity, advertising.
(1973)

Aura Enterprises, Inc (Aura Prod.) (213) 656-9373
7911 Willoughby Ave, Los Angeles 90046
F/V: principally religious documentaries. Record and
cassette production; specialty is Indian (Eastern)
music. Richard Bock, pres. (1971/2)

Aurora Productions   (213) 275-4007
9606 Santa Monica Blvd, Beverly Hills 90210
F: features, including Eddie and the Cruisers, Heart
Like a Wheel.

Bruce Austin Productions   (213) 462-4844
6110 Santa Monica Blvd, Los Angeles 90038
F/V: documentaries and shorts. Film transfer (16mm
to Super 8); videotape editing: 3/4 inch off line,
on line. (1972/3)

The Avalon Group   (213) 652-6654
8833 Sunset Blvd, Suite 302, Los Angeles 90069
F: features, documentaries, music. Package and develop. Frank Naft, president.

Avanti Films   (213) 465-3168
6855 Santa Monica Blvd, Los Angeles 90038
F/V: educational and documentary films on prejudice,
EEO/Affirmative Action, substance abuse (especially
alcoholism), health; for schools, industry, government. Jeff Miller. Production arm of Motivational
Media/Max Miller. (1965/8)

AVRAD   (213) 413-1181
2510 Sunset Blvd, Los Angeles 90026
Video production; facilities and stage.
Richard Gray, technical director.

Azurite Productions   (213) 621-2700
305 Boyd St, Los Angeles 90013
V: educational, documentary, and B&I. Caters to artists and art galleries. Studio facilities. (1976/2)

B

Jacques Bailhe   (213) 466-5544
1250 n. Crescent Heights, Los Angeles 90046
F/V: commercials, documentaries (including Cattle-
Drive); packaging of literary properties. Jacques
Bailhe, poducer. (1979/6)

Bob Baker Productions   **(213) 250-9995**
1345 W. First St, Los Angeles 90026
Puppet and marionette films, both in-house and working with other producers for puppet segments. Sets, props, special effects. Principal business is marionette shows. Bob Baker, general manager; Tina Gainsboro, production director. (1950/20)

Bandera Enterprises   **(818) 985-5050**
P O Box 1107, Studio City 91604
F/V: TV series (and worldwide distribution), commercials, health films. Don Flagg, pres. (1945/6)

Bob Banner Associates   **(213) 657-6800**
8687 Melrose Ave. #M-20, Los Angeles 90069
F/V: TV series, specials (including Perry Como specials), and features. (1960/15)

Barmeier & Company   **(818) 841-9294**
PO Box 492, Burbank 91503
Production company developing projects for film, TV, and cable; seeking projects in those areas. Financing. Bob Barmeier, Michael Chiz, Terry Lynn.

Barnard Productions   **(213) 454-3552**
747 Via de La Paz, Pacific Palisades 90272
Music video, commercials, industrials. Post production of features. Michael Barnard, owner/dir.

Barr Films   **(818) 681-6978**
P O Box 5567, Pasadena 91107
Production and distribution: shorts for education, management & training. Donald Barr, pres; Mark Chodzko, producer; John Dyas, marketing.

Barry & Enright Productions   **(213) 556-1000**
1888 Century Park East #1100, Los Angeles 90067
F: TV specials, features (including Private Lessons), and TV series: Jokers Wild (Allen Koss, prod), Tic Tac Dough (Chris Sahl, prod).

Hall Bartlett Productions   **(213) 278-8883**
9200 Sunset Blvd, Suite 908, Los Angeles 90069
F: features, including Love Is Forever. (1956/5)

Barton Production   **(213) 464-8381, 838-9183**
3667 Overland Ave #11, Los Angeles 90034
F: features. (1984/1)

Saul Bass/Herb Yager and Associates   (213) 466-9701
7089 Sunset Blvd, Los Angeles 90028
F: features, commercials, shorts. (1956/35)

Bassinson Productions   (213) 466-2171
937 N. Cole, Hollywood 90038
Commercials. Oscar Bassinson, dir.; Harvey Warren, exec prod.

Batjac Productions   (213) 278-9870
9570 Wilshire Blvd, Beverly Hills 90212
F: features. Michael Wayne, president. (1951)

BBZ Films   (213) 399-7793
321 Hampton Dr #209, Venice 90291
Development of feature and TV film projects. Bill Benenson, general partner; Bill Mar, vp, story department; John Wentworth, project director; Phyllis Benenson, producer.

Chris Bearde Productions   (213) 394-9606
225 Santa Monica Blvd, Santa Monica 90401
V: TV series, features. (1976/5)

Warren Beatty   (213) 468-5870
5555 Melrose Ave, Hollywood 90038
Director-producer of features, including Reds.

Rolland Beech Productions   (619) 323-8413
27-500 Avenida Quintana, Palm Springs 92264
F/V: TV series, commercials, shorts; stage productions for cable and PBS; sports. Aerial (helicopter) cinematography. Studio & editorial facilities. Rolland Beech, exec producer. (1975)

Dave Bell Associates, Inc (DBA)   (213) 851-7801
3211 Cahuenga Blvd West, Hollywood 90068
F/V: features (including Do You Remember Love?), mini-series, documentaries (including Missing...Have You Seen This Person?), and TV series (including Alive & Well, On Campus). Rental of facilities, equipment; post production. Dave Bell, exec prod; prod: James Thompson, Wayne Threm. (1969/50)

Cal Bernstein Productions   (213) 461-3737
672 S. Lafayette Park Pl, Los Angeles 90057
F: features, commercials, shorts. See: Dove Films

10

The Bernstein Company (213) 461-5100
1124 N. Citrus Ave, Los Angeles 90038
F/V: commercials. Jordan Bernstein, director; Dan
Lindquist, director; Finn Myggen, exec prod; Bill
Bloom, production coord; Sally Bernstein, office
mgr; Charles Kirkwood, representative.

Bert, Barz & Kirby (213) 462-7261
1956 N. Cahuenga Blvd, Los Angeles 90068
Creation, production of humorous radio & TV commercials. Partners: Bert Berdis, Alan Barzman, Jim
Kirby.

Best International Films, Inc (213) 550-7311
9200 Sunset Blvd, Penthouse 22, Los Angeles 90069
Feature distribution.

Beverly Hills Screening, Inc (213) 275-3088
8949 Sunset Blvd, #201, Los Angeles 90069
F/V: animation, special effects; motion control,
lasers, emphasis upon new technologies. Jon Edwards,
pres. Distribution also. Associated company: The
Beverly Hills Screening Room: 16 & 35mm.
(1977/5)

BGP Productions,Inc (818) 506-4925
10637 Burbank Blvd, North Hollywood 91601
Independent motion picture production. Morgan Paull,
pres; Don Galloway, CEO; Mike Frankovich Jr, production; Debby Duffy, vp; Ron Lewis, financial officer;
A. Micheal Pascal, dir. operations.

Jerry Bick Productions, Inc (818) 906-3137
3506 Coy Dr, Sherman Oaks CA 91423
F: features, including Swing Shift, Against All Odds
(1967/1)

Big Time Picture Co (213) 207-0921
12210 1/2 Nebraska Ave, Los Angeles 90025
35mm Kem editorial supplies & rental. ACMADE code-
master (35mm). Edge coating service. Susan Klos
Dolan, pres; Dennis Dolan. (1978/4)

Tony Bill See: Market Street Productions 396-5937

Blalack & Company see Praxis (818) 508-0402

11

Daniel H. Blatt Productions   (818) 954-4483
4000 Warner Blvd. Producer 7 Suite 3, Burbank 91522
F/TV: TV programing and features.

Blenco Inc   (213) 271-1709
340 S. Oakhurst, Beverly Hills 90212
Writing, packaging of features, industrials, and documentaries. Leonard Neubauer, pres.

Thoms Bliss   (213) 473-6690
PO Box 24C71, Los Angeles 90024
Film and videotape production. Thomas Bliss, producer/director. DGA, numerous film & TV credits.

Gary Blohm Productions   (213) 457-3228
PO Box 4248, Malibu 90265
TV production, also film. Gary Blohm, pres.

Blondheim Productions   (213) 467-5316
6060 Sunset Blvd, Hollywood 90028
F: documentaries, commercials, B&I, education. (1970)

Blue Andre Productions,Inc   (818) 760-2110
12711 Ventura Blvd #301, Studio City 91604
Producer.

Blue Dolphin Productions   (213) 467-7660
650 N. Bronson Ave, Hollywood 90004
Music for film, scoring, efx, records. Music supervision, transfers (35mag 16 mag). Contracting for musicians for film, on camera, sideline. Bruce Langhorne, pres; Morgan Cavett, vp.

The Blum Group, Inc   (213) 476-2229
494 Tuallitan Rd, Los Angeles 90049
F: features; produce, arrange finance, and distribute (theatrical, pay TV, and foreign). (1973).

Stanford Blum Enterprises   (818) 501-3555
4222 Woodman Ave, Sherman Oaks 91423
F/V: features, commercials, TV series, shorts. Specialties: music video and promotions for record industry; sports. (1973/4)

Lin Bolen Productions   (213) 456-1339
19706 Pacific Coast Hwy, Malibu 90265
F/V: TV series and features. (1975/2)

12

Bonjo Productions, Ltd   **(213) 426-3622**
1 Transglobal Sq., Box 7005, Long Beach 90807-0005
F/V: features and TV series and miniseries. Dr. J.
Bond Johnson, CEO, exec. prod.; Frank Capra Jr,
exec. prod.; Travis E. Pike, production; Rudolph
Maglin vp, business affairs.

Seymour Borde & Associates   **(213) 461-3986**
1800 N. Highland, Hollywood 90028
F: features, including Hollywood Hot Tubs. Seymour
Borde, pres; Mark Borde, vp. (1960/5)

Boss Film Corp/Entertain. Effects Grp (213) 823-0433
13335 Maxella Ave, Marina Del Rey 90292
Visual effects for motion pictures including Ghost-
busters. Richard Edlund, visual effects supervis;
George Mather, production supervis.

Boston Productions   **(818) 348-9216**
5430 Paradise Valley Rd, Hidden Hills 91302
TV movies, pilots, series. Joe Boston, producer.

Bosustow Studios   **(213) 450-3936**
1649 Eleventh St, Santa Monica 90404
F: animation studio; some live action. TV, commercials, educational; laser discs and interactive
discs for arcades and video games. (1967/28)

Zev Braun Pictures   **(213) 659-8032**
PO Box 36M69, Los Angeles CA 90036
F: features, mini-series for TV; including Where are
the Children, Marlene. Chet Walker, production.
(1966/5)

Braverman Productions   **(213) 466-4111**
6290 Sunset Blvd, Hollywood CA 90028
F/V: TV specials, documentaries, documentaries, features, B&I, title sequences. Programs include Comic
of the Month. Kinestasis animation. Charles
Braverman, pres-ex producer-dir; Ted Herrmann, post-
product. dir; David Fudge, prod. mgr. (1970/10)

Bravo Productions   **(213) 855-0708**
947 Hilldale Ave, Los Angeles 90069
Development of screenplays, budgets; pre-prod and
production of commercials, promos, shorts, and features. Marino Colmano, producer/director.

BRB Entertainment   **(213) 652-4422**
666 N. Robertson Blvd, Los Angeles 90069
F/V: TV series, features, specials including Diana
Ross in Central Park, 35th Annual Emmy Awards. Associated personal management company: BRB Management.
(1975/11)

Martin Bregman Productions, Inc   **(818) 508-4950**
100 Universal City Plaza, Universal City 91608
Independent feature production. Martin Bregman,
chairman; Louis Stroller, vice chairman; Martin
Caan, president; Barbara Louis-Marco, VP creative
affairs, NY phone: (212) 421-6161

Broadwood Productions   **(213) 552-9247**
2029 Century Park East #1140, Los Angeles 90067
F: features. Also distribution to television. Harold
Goldman, pres; Marvin Cole, sec/treas. (1979)

Brookfield Productions   **(213) 390-9767**
11600 Washington Place #203, Los Angeles 90066
TV and film production. Exec. prods: Fern Field,
Norman Brooks; Barbara Klein, development; Aaron
Leider, director of features; Michael Slater, pro-
duction coordinator.

Brooksfilms Ltd   **(213) 203-1375**
10201 W. Pico Blvd, Los Angeles 90035
F: features including Frances, My Favorite Year. Mel
Brooks.

Howard Brown & Associates   **(213) 553-8561**
c/o Progressive Artists
400 S. Beverly Dr, Beverly Hills CA 90212
F: features, including Cheech and Chong comedies.
Howard Brown, pres. (1978)

The Bryna Company   **(213) 274-5294**
141 El Camino Dr, Suite 209, Beverly Hills 90212
F: features, including Draw. Kirk Douglas, pres.
(1958/5)

Bill Burrud Productions, Inc   **(213) 937-0300**
1100 S. La Brea Ave, Los Angeles 90019
F/V: features, documentaries, TV series. Specialty:
wildlife subjects. (1954)

Gene Burson-Filmcrafters (213) 641-6028
P O Box 45572, Los Angeles 90045
F/V/Multimedia: documentaries, commercials, B&I;
live action, animation. No internally financed production. (1968)

Bustles Productions (818) 980-2924
11634 Moorpark, Studio City 91602
Commercials: production & casting. Kathleen Fisher,
owner.

Ken Butler Productions (213) 469-6955
6305 Yucca St #501, Hollywood 90028
Threatical production including Requiem for a Heavy-
weight (NY). Ken Butler, pres.

Caruth C. Byrd Productions,Inc (818) 985-5015
11741 Brookdale Lane, North Hollywod 91604
F/V: features including Hollywood High II, commer-
cials. Distribution through Lone Star Pictures.
Caruth C. Byrd, chairman; Don Averitt, pres; Cotton
Whittington, vp. (1965/18)

C & D

Cabala Communications, Inc (213) 461-7825
6565 Sunset Blvd, Hollywood 90028
V: TV specials for pay TV; world syndication. Riff
Markowitz, pres; Jeff Loeb, production. (1974/4)
See: Markowitz/Chesler

Cactus Tree Productions (213) 466-2825
6123 Glen Oak, Los Angeles 90068
F: features. The company discourages calls from
prospective employees as all production personnel
are obtained through the trades.

Calico Ltd.   **(818) 885-6663**
8843 Shirley Ave, Northridge 91324
Full production facility: animation, special effects, computer graphics, and live action. Lee Mann, pres. exec prod; Tom Burton vp, prod/dir; directors: Claudia Z Burton, Ken Leonard, Joel Fajnor.

California Communications   **(213) 466-8511**
6900 Santa Monica Blvd, Hollywood 90038
Rental equipment (Betacam & Recam Video) and post production facilites. Sub-producer with crews. Bill Muster, owner; Michael Brauin, vp rental mgr. (1974/15)

Cal-Vista International   **(818) 780-9000**
6649 Odessa, Van Nuys 91406
F/V: adult features. Associated company: Cal-Vista Video. Sidney Niekerk, pres. (1965/20)

Cambridge Films   **(213) 203-8488**
324 Beverly Dr. #205, Beverly Hills 90212
F: technical films about horses and cows for veterinary schols. Also distributor. Paul Guerin, pres. (1966)

Stephen J. Cannell Productions   **(213) 465-5800**
7083 Hollywood Blvd, Hollywood 90028
F: TV series, including The A-Team, Riptide, Hardcastle & McCormick, Hunter. Stephen Cannell, exec producer; Jo Swerling, Jr, supervising prod.

Cannon Films, Inc   **(213) 469-8124**
6464 Sunset Blvd. #1150, Los Angeles 90028
F: features, including Hercules, Revenge of the Ninja. Menahem Golan, chairman; Yoram Globus, pres. (1967/35)

The Carlin Company   **(213) 652-9354**
8721 Sunset Blvd #208, Los Angeles 90069
F: features. Edward Carlin, pres. (1971/2)

Mark Carliner Productions, Inc   **(818) 763-4783**
11700 Laurelwood Dr, Studio City 91604
F: TV series and features including The Phoenix. Mark Carliner, exec producer. (1976/3)

Carman Productions (213) 873-7370
15456 Cabrito Road, Van Nuys 91406
Produces records, TV specials, and features. Joe
Gottfried, Tom Skeeter, Mark Levy

Allan Carr Enterprises (213) 278-2490
P O Box 691670, Los Angeles 90069
F/V: features, including Cloak & Dagger, Where the
Boys Are. Also live theatre, including La Cage Aux
Folles. Allan Carr, pres-director-producer. (1966/5)

The William Carruthers Company (213) 465-0669
200 N. Larchmont, Los Angeles 90004
V: TV series, specials, game shows including Press
Your Luck. (1969/2)

Carson Cable TV Company (213) 515-7979
20930 Bonita Ave. #Z, Carson 90746
Cable franchise with local origination. Dan
McMullin, public access director.

Carson Productions Group (818) 506-5333
10045 Riverside Dr, Toluca Lake CA 91602
T/V: television programing. John J. McMahon, president.

Carson Films (818) 506-5333
10045 Riverside Dr, Toluca Lake CA 91602
F: features. Richard Fischoff, pres; Terri
Farnsworth, vp-development; Kathy Rowe, story editor.

Jack Cash Productions (213) 462-5885
650 N. Bronson Ave, Los Angeles 90004
Manufacturers production boards. UPM/AD on features,
TV series, MOW. Produces commercials, documentaries,
shorts.

Cassiopeia Productions (213) 659-9709
968 Larrabee, Los Angeles CA 90069
F/V: TV series for cable. Valen Watson. (1982/4)

Castle Combe Productions, Inc (213) 551-0588
1147 S. Beverly Dr. #B, Los Angeles 90035
4142 Benedict Canyon, Sherman Oaks 91423
F/V: TV series, including That's Hollywood, features, and TV specials. David Lawrence pres; Adam
Lawrence, development. (1975,7)

Catalina Production Group　　　　　(818) 954-4335
2901 W. Alameda #650, Burbank 91505
Features, programing for cable; stage productions.
Producers: Franklin Levy, Gregory Harrison; Matthew
Rushton, co-prod; Paul Nagle, development; Jeanne
Troy, theatre co-producer.

Cathedral Films　　　　　　　　(818) 991-3290
PO Box 4029, Westlake Village 91359
F/V/FS: religious education. Pres: Rev. James L.
Friedrich; A. Scott Miller, exec vp.

CBS (Columbia Broadcasting System)

CBS Entertainment　　　　　　(213) 852-2345
Television City, 7800 Beverly Bl, Los Angeles 90036
Bud Grant, pres. TV series include: Twilight Zone.
Development: Steve Mills, vp, TV movies-miniseries;
Michael Ogiens vp, comedy; Carla Singer, vp, drama.

CBS Productions
Alan Levin, pres.

CBS/MTM　　　　　　　　　　(818) 760-5000
4024 Radford, Studio City 91604
17 sound stages. Joint operation with MTM.

Centre Films, Inc　　　　　　(213) 466-5123
1103 N. El Centro Ave, Hollywood 90038
F/V: commercials, TV, B&I, health, educational.
Also distributes childbirth education films. Winter
D. Horton, Jr, pres; (1970/7)

Century Distributors　　　　　(818) 781-0177
16153 Cohasset St, Van Nuys 91406
F/V: adult features and shorts. Principally distributor Arrow films & Deep Throat.

Century Video Corporation　　　(213) 550-7444
280 S. Beverly Dr #501, Beverly Hills 90212
Exec. producers of programs for the videocassette
industry, and commercial tV and cable worldwide.
Lawrence Scheer, chairman; Steve Baker, vp finance;
Sandra Turbow, secretary.

John Cestare Productions, Inc   **(213) 659-4134**
P O Box 5286, Beverly Hills 90210
F/V: features, TV series, and shorts. John Cestare, pres. (1961/15)

Challenge Productions, Inc   **(213) 225-4712**
469 N. Crescent #2537, Beverly Hills CA 90213
Challenge is an Alaska corportation that finances and produces features. Local office coordinates staff and post production for shooting in Alaska. Kenneth Ott, exec director. (1978/4)

Ernest Chambers Productions, Inc   **(213) 464-6158**
1438 N. Gower St. Box 44, Hollywood 90028
V: TV series and features, including 99 Ways to Attract the Right Man. (1975/3)

B. G. Charles, Inc   **(213) 273-3283**
9291 Flicker Place, Los Angeles 90069
F: feature trailers, commercials for radio/TV. Feature promotion service. (1960/12)

Chartoff-Winkler Productions, Inc   **(213) 204-0474**
10125 W. Washington Blvd, Culver City 90230
F: features including The Right Stuff. Robert Chartoff; Irwin Winkler. (1967)

R. B. Chenoweth Films   **(213) 691-1652**
P O Box 233, La Habra 90631
F/V: B&I shorts. RBC Enterprises rents 16mm & 35mm flatbed editing equipment. (1955/2)

Chinese World Television, Inc   **(213) 488-9122-4**
1101 W. 7th St, Los Angeles 90017
F/V: Chinese TV programing; features, commercials, TV series. Overseas production service and Kung Fu shorts. Broadcasting arm: KSCI, Channel 18. Affiliates in San Francisco and N.Y. Tuen-ping Yang, gen manager. (1983/9)

Chip Enterprises, Inc   **(213) 208-2111**
11811 W. Olympic Blvd, Los Angeles 90064
V: TV series and specials. Woody Fraser, pres. (1965/12)

Chrisan Productions (213) 393-9797
210 25th St, Santa Monica 90402
Producer of documentaries, sales films, and commercials in US and overseas. Stanton Korey, pres.

Damon Christian, Inc (818) 760-8877
11440 Chandler Blvd, #1100, North Hollywood 91601
F/V: low budget theatrical and TV features. (1965/8)

Churchill Films (213) 657-5110
662 N. Robertson Blvd, Los Angeles 90069
F/V: educational films, documentaries (including Down for the Count) ; also distribution- to schools, libraries,and hospitals. George McQuilkin, pres; Robert Churchill, vp and Chairman; Bob Glore, sales; Jim Churchill, marketing.

Michael Cimino See: Sweetwater Prod. (818) 954-1691

Cineguild Productions, Inc 461-2721
1015 N. Cahuenga Blvd, Los Angeles 90038
F/V: TV series, features, shorts. Dialogue and sound editing; post production facilities. (1979/4)

Cinema Group, Inc (213) 204-0102
8758 Venice Blvd, Los Angeles 90034
F: features. Harry E. Gould, Jr, pres; Venetia Stellvenson, vp, production; Richard James, exec vp. (1979/9)

Cinema Samples Productions (213) 932-8161
1545 Point View St, Los Angeles 90035
F/V: commercials, B&I films. Kermit Samples, director; Betty Fox, marketing. (1975) 2nd Phone: 932-4161

The Cinesphere Corporation (213) 221-6043
2443 Lillyvale Ave, Los Angeles 90032
F: production services; special effects and 2nd-unit production for features, TV, commercials. Byron Bauer. (1978/8)

Cinaco Film Company (213) 278-3302
9056 Santa Monica Blvd #200, Los Angeles 90069
Motion picture production and distribution. Fred Briskin, pres, exec prod; Tenny Chonin, dir operations; Marc Zavat, prod; John Tremaine, research and development.

20

Bob Clampett Productions, Inc   **(213) 466-0264**
729 Seward St, Los Angeles 90038
F: animated commercials and cartoons; specialty is
animation and puppetry. (1949)

Dick Clark Productions   **(818) 841-3003**
3003 W. Olive Ave, Burbank 91505
Dick Clark Cinema Productions, Inc (features), Dan
Paulson; Dick Clark TV Productions, Inc (TV programs
and series), Al Schwartz; Dick Clark Concepts, Inc
(live concerts); Fran La Maina, in charge of production for corporate group.

Woody Clark Productions   **(415) 777-1668**
943 Howard Street, San Francisco 94103
F/V: documentaries, features, business shorts.
Woodrow W. Clark Jr, pres/exec prod; Tom Quinn,
story editor; Stacey Foiles, production superv.
(1979/6)

Clean Slate Productions   **(818) 845-0860**
231 N. Beachwood Dr, Burbank 91506
F/V productions. Also videos for wills, depositions,
and other legal and personal purposes. Dan Fendel,
pres; Scot Fraley vp.

Steve Clements   **(213) 856-1050**
5746 Sunset Blvd, Los Angeles 90028
Producer: Hour TV-magazine; Martin Berman, exec
producer. (1980/40)

Cloutier, Inc   **(213) 655-1263**
704 N. Gardner Ave, #6, Los Angeles 90046
Pre production services. Chantall Cloutier, owner.
(1978/1)

Coast Productions   **(213) 876-2021**
1001 N. Poinsettia Place, Hollywood 90046
F/V: commercials. Jack Yopp, chairman; Jay Grandy,
pres; Patrick Collins, gen manager.

Coast Special Effects   **(818) 762-1182**
4907 N. Lankershim Bl, N. Hollywood 91601
Special effects for commercials, movies, trailers,
and corporate communications. Phil Kellison, creative director.

Harold Cohen Productions   **(213) 550-0570**
9200 Sunset Blvd, Los Angeles 90069
Personal management. F: features, TV series.

Herman Cohen Productions, Inc   **(213) 466-3388**
650 N. Bronson Ave, Los Angeles 90004
F: features. Distributing company: Cobra Media.
Didier Chatelain, vp. (1958)

The Colman Group   **(213) 466-0700**
6363 Sunset Blvd #711, Hollywood 90028
TV: fashion and music videos. Joel Colman, dirctor;
Rene Eram, director; Katy Bishop, exec prod; John
Clark, prod; Kris Parker, production mgr.

Columbia Pictures Productions   **(818) 954-6000**
Columbia Plaza, Burbank 91505
F: features. Development personnel; Wendie Margolis;
Robert Lawrence.

Columbia Television
F/V: TV programing, including T.J. Hooker, Crazy
Like a Fox, Lime Street, Stir Crazy; The Young and
the Restless, Days of Our Lives. Development personnel: Richard Heller, comedy; Rachel Tabori, drama;
Susan Simons, daytime; Andrew Hill, MOW, mini-series
& variety.

The Commercial Store   **(213) 470-2851**
10844 Rochester Ave, Los Angeles 90024
F/V: commercials, B&I. Michael Dean, pres; John
Gilbert, marketing. (1971/5)

Companionway Films   **(818) 508-3381**
100 Universal City Plaza, Universal City 91608
TV and motion picture writing and production. T.S.
Cook, pres.

Compass International Pictures   **(213) 859-4867**
9229 Sunset Blvd. #610, Los Angeles 90069
F: features; distribution, including cable TV.
Irwin Yablans, producer.

Con Artists Productions   **(213) 938-9436**
7471 Melrose Ave. #22, Los Angeles 90046
F: features. Associate company: Con Artists: publicity and promotion company. (1981/4)

Michael Conte Productions   (213) 467-0207
12319 19th Helena Dr, Brentwood 90049
F/V: education, industry, features.

Corday Productions, Inc   (818) 954-2637
Columbia Plaza East, Burbank 91505
V: TV series, including Days of Our Lives. Producers: Ken Corday, Shelley Curtis; assoc. prod: Beth Milstein; Al Rabin, supervising exec. producer; Mrs. Ted Corday, exec. prod; Becky Greenlaw, assoc. prod. (1950/50)

Corporate Productions, Inc   (818) 760-2622
4516 Mariota, Toluca Lake 91602
F: documentaries and B&I. (1970/10)

Pierre Cossette Productions, Inc   (213) 278-3366
8899 Beverly Blvd, #900, Los Angeles 90048
V: syndicated television series including Salute.

Cotler & Brothers Productions   (818) 908-9333
14746 Archwood Blvd, Van Nuys 91405
Screen writing and music production for flim/tape projects. (1975/4)

The Cousteau Society, Inc   (213) 656-4422
8440 Santa Monica Blvd, Los Angeles 90069
Post-production film work on Jacques Cousteau's documentaries. John Soh, editor, assoc. producer. (1977/2)

Creative Artists Productions   (213) 876-2939
1134 N. Formosa Ave, Los Angeles 90046
F/V: documentaries, especially in archaeology and biblical themes; also writing. Ralph B. Fletcher, pres. (1973/1)

Creative Communications, Inc   (213) 823-4225
13900 Panay Way M120, Marina del Rey 90292
F: B&I, and educational. (1968/4)

Creative Enterprises International   (213) 463-9929
6630 Sunset Blvd, Hollywood 90028
F/V: commercials, films, and promotions, especially for Japan. Akiko Agishi, pres, exec prod. (1972/9)

Crest Film Distributors, Inc (213) 652-8844
116 N. Robertson Blvd. #701, Los Angeles 90048
Distribution of features to theatres. Jerry Persell,
pres; Gary Persell, sales manager. (1961/7)

Crossover Programming Company (213) 451-9762
6290 Sunset Blvd, Hollywood CA 90028
Original programing for pay TV. See: Braverman Productions. (1983)

CRM Productions, Inc (213) 870-5912
2999 Overland Ave #211, Los Angeles CA 90064
F: B&I, education. (1977/8)

Crown International Pictures (213) 657-6700
292 S. La Cienega Blvd, Beverly Hills 90211
F: features. Primarily distributor; international
distribution through Crown International Exports
Corporation. (1978/20)

The Crystal Juke Box Film Corporation (213) 395-3098
P O Box 2011, Beverly Hills 90212
F: features. (1974/2)

CTA Film Productions (818) 992-1304
23730 Clarendon St, Woodland Hills 91367
F: animation. TV cartoons, commercials, shorts for
B&I, education, government.

Cumberland Mountain Film Company (213) 396-4543
620 Lincoln Blvd, Venice 90291
F: features, special projects, subcontracted specialties. William R. Murrow, pres.

Cally Curtis Company (213) 467-1101
1111 N. Las Palmas Ave, Hollywood 90038
F/V: producer and distributor of training films,
shorts, commercials. Cally Curtis, pres/director;
Kathy Know, adminis./product. manager. (1957/5)

Dan Curtis Productions, Inc (213) 557-6910
9911 W. Pico Blvd, Los Angeles 90035
F/V: TV series and features, including The Winds of
War. Distribution through Dan Curtis Distrib. Corp.
Dan Curtis, pres. (1960/8)

Cypress Point Productions   (818) 954-1382
4000 Warner Blvd, Producer's One #210, Burbank 91505
F: features including Florence Nightingale. Gerald
Abrams, pres; Jennifer Faulstich, vp development;
Chris Rubin. (1978)

D Productions   (213) 273-6508
801 N. Rexford Dr, Beverly Hills 90210
Production, writing, editing, critiquing screenplays. Ms Dale A. Engelson, pres.

Dana Productions   (213) 877-9246
6249 Babcock Ave, N. Hollywood 91606
F: shorts; producer-distributor; including films
relating to self-esteem, drug & alcohol rehabilita-
tion; some Spanish, some captioned. Albert Saparoff,
pres-prod. (1970/5)

Dateline Communications   (213) 393-9494
1255 Lincoln Blvd, #300, Santa Monica 90401
V: 5% commercials, 10% industrials, 80% documentaries, 5% specials. Frank Widder, dir; Liliane
Pelzman, assoc dir; Bill Widder exec prod. (1983/8)

Dave & Dave, Inc   (818) 508-7738
1765 N. Highland Ave #226, Hollywood 90078
F/V: commercials, B&I. Also radio commercials. Dave
Darmour & Dave Sebastian Williams. (1983/3)

Davis/Panzer Productions, Inc   (213) 463-2343
1438 N. Gower #174, Los Angeles 90028
F: features including The Osterman Weekend. Peter
Davis; William Panzer.

The Debin-Locke Company   462-2608
1119 N. McCadden Place, Hollywood 90038
F: features including A Gun in the House. (1979/5)

deFaria Productions, Inc   275-9392
427 N. Canon Dr, Beverly Hills 90210
F/V: features including Don't Cry It's Only Thunder,
and TV series. (970/2)

Delaney Films   (805) 653-2699
P O Box 363, Ventura 93002
F: specialist in surfing and ocean sports; works
with agencies for commercials. Bill Delaney, dir;
Victoria Montague, producer. (1975/3)

Harry De Ligter Productions   (213) 450-5324
2258 Twentieth St, Santa Monica 90405
F/V: features, shorts for B&I and education. Harry
De Ligter, pres. (1977)

Deliverance Productions   (818) 954-2533
4000 Warner Blvd, Bungalow 25, Burbank 91522
F: features. Burt Reynolds; Hank Moonjean.

Delta Productions   (213) 463-3582 (46-DELTA)
3333 Glendale Blvd #3, Los Angeles 90039
Full service production company; editing; negative
cutting, sound, dry laboratory, sound effects. Specializes in rush work. Stock footage. Brian King,
owner; Ted Sawicki, editor, coffee maker.

Dennis, Guy, & Hirsch   (213) 854-6311
616 W. Bourne, Los Angeles 90069
F/V: commercials. Steve Marvin, exec. producer.
Office in N.Y.

Hal Dennis Productions   (213) 467-7146
6314 La Mirada, Los Angeles 90038
Rental for editorial (16 & 35) equipment.

DeSort Films   (213) 822-2400
2017 Pacific Ave, Vencie 90291
F: commercials. Linda Stewart (LA). Robyn Bensinger,
exec prod. (1979)

Laurence Deuthsch Design/Productions (213) 937-3521
751 N. Highland Ave, Hollywood 90038
F: corporate and documentary films; 16/35mm post
production. Laurence Deutsch, director; Sherry
Pringle, prod, production manager; Bill Nash, production coordinator.

Devi Productions   (213) 552-7878
9911 W Pico Blvd. #1550, Los Angeles 90035
F: features.

Diamond P Sports   (818) 702-9723
21130 Costanso, Woodland Hills CA 91364
V: TV programs and series; especially sports (including American Sports Cavalcade). (1980/3)

Dibie-Dash Productions   **(213) 663-1955**
4974 Hollywood Blvd, Hollywood 90028
F: documentaries, B&I, education. George Dibie,
pres. (1964/5)

Dimension Films   **(213) 657-2910**
666 N. Robertson Blvd, Los Angeles 90069
F/FS: B&I and education. Gary Goldsmith, pres.
(1962/2)

The Directors Network   **(213) 461-0363**
2242 Cahuenga Blvd, Hollywood 90038
Agent: TV commercial director. Steve Lewis, pres.

Walt Disney Productions   **(818) 840-1000**
500 S. Buena Vista St, Burbank 91521
Richard Frank, president. Corporate divisions:

Walt Disney Motion Pictures & TVB (features & network TV) Jeffrey Katzenberg, chairman. Development:
Ricardo Mestres, vp; David Hoberman, vp; Jane
Rosenthal. Television syndication: Bob Jacquemin,
vp. Television development: Grant Rosenberg, vp.

Walt Disney Channel (cable channel) Peggy
Christianson, vp, programing.

Other divisions: Buena Vista Distributing, Buena
Vista International, Walt Disney Telecommunications,
Walt Disney Educational Media, Walt Disney World.

Documentary Productions, Inc   **(818) 282-0420**
612 E. Ross St, Alhambra 91801
F/V:B&I, features. Distributor of racing films.
(1966/2)

Dolph'n Productions   **(213) 399-9148**
2525 Main St #204, Santa Monica CA 90405
F: options and develops material for features and TV
represented by Creative Artists Agency. Exec prods:
Randolph Williams, William Urbany; Fern Baum, assoc
prod, development.

Domino Productions, Inc   **(213) 552-2204**
2049 Century Park East, Los Angeles 90067
F/V: TV series, cable, features. Finance and produce. John Schwartz, dir creative affairs. (1979/10)

Don-El Productions, Ltd (213) 856-1014
5746 Sunset Blvd, Los Angeles 90028
V: TV series and pilots including syndication of Too
Close for Comfort. Bob Stolfi, development.

Larry Dorn Associates (213) 935-6266
5550 Wilshire Blvd, Los Angeles 90036
F/V: TV series. Stock library (offices in London,
Paris, Cape Town): time-lapse & special effects a
specialty. TV and feature tie-ins. Linda Dorn, film
library.

Michael Douglas Productions (213) 203-1595
10201 W. Pico Blvd, Los Angeles 90035
F: features including Romancing the Stone, Jewel of
the Nile. Michael Douglas, actor, producer; Jane
Kagan, vp creative affairs.

Kirk Douglas See: Bryna Company 274-5294

Dove Films, Inc (213) 461-3737
722 N. Seward St, Los Angeles 90038
Cal Bernstein, director; Sven Nykuist, director/cam-
eraman. See: Cal Bernstein Productions. (1966)

Victor Drai Productions (213) 558-6951
10202 W. Pico Bl, Tracy Bdg 1 fl, Culver City 90230
F: production company. Victor Drai, prod; Kathyrn
McArdle, vp, creative affairs.

Dudley Ltd (818) 797-9778
2408 N. Lake St, Altadena CA 91001
F: travel films. Also distribution. Dudley Warner,
pres; David James, vp. (1954/4)

Dury Associates (213) 461-3617
741 Cahuenga Blvd, Los Angeles 90038
Editorial service for commercials, trailers, shorts.
(1975/5)

The DXTR's (213) 462-6410
6140 Hollywood Blvd, Hollywood 90028
F/V: commercials. Jill Dexter, exec producer; directors: Ron Dexter, George Gage; Kathy Francis,
sales rep. (1966/1)

E

The Eagle Eye Film Company   **(818) 506-6100**
4019 Tujunga Ave, PO Box 1345, Studio City 91604
16 & KEM 35mm editing equipment and rooms. (1970/6)

Ecumedia   **(213) 380-0460**
4270 W. 6th St #10, Los Angeles 90020
Not a production company. Part of the Southern CA
Ecumenical Council; represents churches in discussion of social justice issues in the media. Rev. Dr.
Maxwell Perrow, exec director.

Edgewood Knoll Corporation   **(213) 202-6700**
10726 McCune Ave, Los Angeles 90034
F/V: commercial production; TV production. Arthur N.
Mele, pres/dir; James Cody, exec prod; Robert Lass,
exec vp; Susi Fern, marketing.

Editel   **(213) 931-1821**
729 N. Highland Ave, Hollywood 90038
V: production & post production; stage & mobile
units. A division of Bell & Howell/Columbia Pictures
Video Services. Vince Lyons, exec vp; Bill Johnson,
gen manager. (1966/20)

Ed-Venture Films   **(213) 261-1885**
1122 Calada St, Los Angeles 90023
Production or consultation regarding packaging,
financing of film, videotape, videodisc, holography.
(1954)

Blake Edwards Entertainment   **(213) 553-6741**
1888 Century Park East (#1616), Los Angeles 90067
Company includes B.E.E. Films, B.E.E. Television,
B.E.E. Theatrical, B.E.E. Records, and The Management Company. Features include The Man Who Loved
Women. Blake Edwards, director-producer-writer. Telex: 674304 Blake Ent USA.

George Edwards Productions   (213) 856-8649
Raleigh Studios, 650 North Bronson, Hollywood 90004
F: features (including Harper Valley PTA) and home
video (The Dracula Tapes). George Edwards, wri-
ter/prod; Tony Crechales, assoc prod; Robert
Shawley, asst to prod.

Ralph Edwards Productions   (213) 462-2212
1717 N. Highland Ave. #1018, Los Angeles 90028
V: game shows and TV series including The People's
Court.

Eggers Films   (213) 856-0060
6345 Fountain Ave, Los Angeles 90028
F: commercials. Director: Bob Eggers; exec prod:
Sterling Ray; sen prod: Amanda Carmel. Sales rep:
LA/Chi Maureen Melvin; Deb Landes (NY). NY office
(212) 751-9044 (1978)

Einfeld & Associates, Inc   (213) 461-3731
1512 N. Las Palmas Ave, Los Angeles 90028
Occasional production; principal business is film
sound service, dailies, reprints, transfers. Extensive sound effects and music library. (1980/3)

Embassy Communications   (213) 553-3600
1901 Avenue of the Stars, Los Angeles 90067
Alan Horn, chairman. Divisions:

Embassy Pictures (feature production & distribution).

Embassy Telelvision   (818) 985-4321
Studio: 1438 N. Gower Ave, Box 27, Los Angeles 90028
Development: 956 Seward St, Los Angeles 90028
(TV series) including Silver Spoons, The Facts of
Life, Who's the Boss, Different Strokes, 227.

Tandem Productions (TV series Different Strokes).
Embassy Telecommunications (syndication & distribution of TV programs).

EmBer Productions   (213) 660-2670
5006 Franklin Ave, Los Angeles 90027
Commercial production company. Emie Amemiya, exec
prod; James Berry, dir; Jerry Brady, dir; Jack
Howard vp production.

EMC Corporation (213) 463-3282
6855 Santa Monica Blvd. #308, Los Angeles 90038
Audio and video-cassette duplication; floppy disk
duplication; A/V shows. Jerome Greenfield, vp;
Deborah A. Sturges, sales director. (1964)

Energy Productions (213) 462-3310
846 N. Cahuenga Blvd, Hollywood 90038
F: commercials; animation & special effects a specialty. Time-lapse stock film library. Louis
Schwartzberg, producer-dir; Jan Ross, producer;
David Helfand, production manager; Carol Meyers,
marketing; Murray Oken, sales dir. (1971/5)

George Englund Enterprises (213) 454-5504
859 Swarthmore Ave, Pacific Palisades 90272
Feature film and TV production. George Englund,
pres; Michael Greenburg, exec vp.

Entertainment Arts, Inc (818) 841-0225
210 N. Pass Ave, Burbank 91505
F/V: features & syndicated TV series; also distribution. Associated company: Radio Arts, Inc: radio
programing. Larry Vanderveen pres. (1979/3)

Entertainment Productions, Inc (213) 456-3143
2210 Wilshire Blvd, Santa Monica CA 90403
F/V: TV series and features. Edward Coe, pres.

EUE/Screen Gems, Ltd (818) 954-3000
3701 Oak St, Burbank 91505
F/V: commercials; B&I. Production facilities include
stages in NY & LA. Jerry Bernstein, Sr, exec vp &
gen manager; Larry DeLeon, exec. producer.
(1960/25).

Robert Evans Productions (213) 468-5855
5555 Melrose Ave, Los Angeles 90038
F: features including Marathon Man, Chinatown.
(1974)

F

Jerry Fairbanks Productions   **(213) 462-1101**
PO Box 38396, Hollywood CA 90038
F: B&I; features. Distributor to AT&T. (1940/10)
Moving to new office soon.

Falcon Cable TV   **(213) 208-8177**
10889 Wilshire Blvd, #1260, Los Angeles 90025
Cable systems throughout the LA area with local
origination channels.

Family Films   **(818) 997-7500**
14622 Lanark St, Panorama City 91402
F/V: religious. Also distribution - in nine languages. Iris Austin, manager. (1946/13)

Family Theatre Productions   **(213) 874-6633**
7201 Sunset Blvd, Los Angeles 90046
F: religious subjects; distribution. Some TV specials. Dennis Roverato, manager; Austin Peterson,
production; Nicholas Royce, film coordinator. Fr.
Peyton, president. (1942/5)

Faret-Lottimer Productions   **(213) 462-0854**
1438 N. Gower St, Hollywood 90028
F: features. Liv Faret & Barclay Lottimer. (1979/5)

Don Fedderson Productions   **(818) 986-3118**
16255 Ventura Blvd #1117, Encino CA 91436
V: TV series and specials. Don Fedderson, chairman.
(1955/10)

The Edward S. Feldman Company   **(213) 203-1882**
P O Box 900, Beverly Hills 90213
F/V: features and miniseries including Charles &
Diana.

Fenady Associates, Inc   **(213) 466-6375**
249 N. Larchmont - #6, Los Angeles 90004
F: features and TV series. (1962/4)

Freddie Fields Productions, Inc   **(213) 558-5411**
10202 W. Washington Blvd, Culver City 90230
F: features. (1974)

Film Center   **(213) 463-6397**
6362 Hollywood Blvd, #306, Los Angeles 90028
F/V: documentaries, commercials, b&I, education.
Film services: Film-o-mation: films from slides or
multimedia. (1970/3)

Film Communicators   **(818) 766-3747**
11136 Weddington, North Hollywood 91601
F/S/V: primarily deals with fire & industrial safe-
ty. Distribution, sales & rental. Ray Jewell, pres;
Sharon Stockwell, operations (1968/12)

Film Consultants   **(818) 982-9876**
7832 Laurel Grove Ave, N. Hollywood 91605
F/V: documentaries, TV specials, B&I. Post production facility; budgeting. Rodney Recor, managing
partner. (1977/1)

Film Core   **(213) 464-7303**
849 N. Seward, Los Angeles 90038
16 & 35mm post production; 3/4 & 1" videotape editing. Larry Chernoff, pres; Charles Chubak & Steve
McCoy, vp. (1971/22)

The Film Group   **(818) 363-7342**
1158 Chimineas, Northridge CA 91326
F/V: B&I, commercials, documentaries, features. Dan
Willis, pres. (1968/3)

Film Impressions. Ltd   **(213) 466-6327**
743 N. Seward St, Hollywood 90038
Motion picture advertising company. (1971/6)

Film Jamel   **(213) 273-7773**
195 S. Beverly Dr, Los Angeles 90212
F/V: animated features. Gilbert Cates.

Film Packages International, Inc   **(213) 274-5251**
9000 Sunset Blvd, #615, Los Angeles 90069
F: features and mini-series. Arnold Kopelson, chairman; Pierre David, pres; Denise Dinovi, vp, creative
affairs.

The Film Place   **(213) 464-0116**
1311 N. Highland, Los Angeles 90028
F/V: post production. Joe Benadon, pres; Phil
Gossart, editor; Sonny Klein, supervisor. (1970/6)

The Film Tree   **(213) 659-9350**
8554 Melrose Ave, Los Angeles 90069
F/V: commercials. Frank Tuttle, exec producer; directors: Ross McCanse, John McShane, Ron Phillips.
(1976)

Film Ventures International   **(818) 769-4210**
11908 Ventura Blvd #201, Studio City 91604
Motion picture distribution and marketing world
wide. One or two in house productions/year. Robert
Steuer, exec vp, marketing; Lawrence Goebel, vp
sales; Jerry Zanitsch, vp, advertising.

Filmart   **(213) 659-7712**
967 N. LaCienega, Los Angeles 90069
Buy/sell motion picture film; 2nd Unit pickup; rental of camera and crews. (1975/5)

Filmation Studios   **(818) 345-7414**
18107 Sherman Way, Reseda 91335
F: animation studio; features, cartoons, TV. Some
live action. Lou Scheimer, pres. (1963/100)

FilmFair   **(818) 877-3191**
10900 Ventura Blvd, Studio City 91604
F/V: commercials. Features, documentaries, educational shorts. Distribution. Offices in NY, Chicago, London. (1960/65)

Filmline Production Associates   **466-8667**
1467 Tamarind Ave, Los Angeles 90028
F: shorts: B&I, documentaries, education, government. Also sales and rental. (1961/10)

Filmrite Associates, inc   **(213) 464-7491**
1040 N. McCadden Place, Los Angeles 90038
F: documentaries.

Financial News Network   **(213) 450-2412**
2525 Ocean Park Blvd, Santa Monica 90405
Cable network; 90 hrs/wk live financial and sports
news; other programs (business and sports) produced
out-of-house. Paul Steinle, pres.; Keith Manasco,
vp, production; Mark Estren, vp, news & programing;
Arnie Rosenthal, vp marketing; Elio Betty, vp sales.

Fine Arts Films, Inc   (818) 506-3683
11632 Ventura Blvd, Studio City 91604
F/V: Animation: children's shows. John Wilson, pres.
(1956/15)

Finnegan Associates   (818) 985-0430, 508-5614
4225 Coldwater Canyon, Studio City 91604
F: features. Bill Finnegan, pres; Pat Finnegan, vp-
producer; Sheldon Pinchek, producer; Margaret
Fannin, production supervisor; Nancy Meyer, develop.

Imero Fiorentino Associates   (213) 467-4020
7060 Hollywood Blvd #1000, Hollywood 90028
Production company specializing in TV series/spe-
cials, industrials; lighting and scenic design.
Robert Dahl, vp production; Nancy Haas, director
production services; Nancy Koester, marketing. NY
office: (212) 246-0600.

First Artists Production Company, Ltd (213) 274-0200
150 El Camino Drive, Beverly Hills 90212
F: features.

Five Star Productions   (714) 852-9115
4600 Campus Dr, Newport Beach 92660
F/V: commercials, B&I. Also known as Five Star Marketing Inc. Bob Kelley, CEO; Mimi Grant, operations.

Flaum-Grinberg Productions   (213) 464-7491
1040 N. McCadden Place, Los Angeles 90038
No new production; distribution of documentary TV
specials. (1960)

Roger Flint Productions, Inc   (213) 851-1060
7758 Sunset Blvd, Los Angeles 90046
F/V: commercials, trailers for features. Story-
boards, music. Susan Turk, exec producer; Roger
Flint, pres-dir. (1975/8)

F-M Motion Picture Services   (818) 849-7618
1811 W. Magnolia Blvd, Burbank 91506
F: B&I. (1950/7)

FMS Productions, Inc   (213) 461-4567
1777 N. Vine St, Los Angeles 90028
Distributor of films on alcoholism and chemical
dependencies. Produces B&I, educational, medical
shorts. (1976/5)

Focus III Productions   **(213) 850-1855**
7805 Sunset Blvd, Hollywood 90046
F/V/M: commercials, shorts. William Goelkel, producer; Tim Everitt, director. (1978/4)

Fontana's Studio   **(818) 997-6985**
5756 Fulton Ave, North Hollywood 91601
Scenic drops, etc. construction for theater, TV,
movies, and amusement parks.

James Forsher Productions   **(213) 461-0178**
650 N. Bronson Ave #108, Hollywood 90004
F: production company.

Foster Bietak Productions   **(818) 788-0120**
13437 Contour Dr, Sherman Oaks 91423
TV and stage production. Prods: Dick Foster, Willy
Bietak; Lynne Foster, assoc prod.

Four D Productions   **(213) 550-7022**
9200 Sunset Blvd #920, Los Angeles 90069
V: syndication of TV series Barney Miller. (1974)

Four Star International, Inc   **(213) 469-2102**
981 N. Cole Ave, Los Angeles CA 90038
F/V: TV series and features; also distribution.
(1955/21)

Sonny Fox Productions   **(213) 650-0606**
1447 N. Kings Road, Los Angeles 90069
F/V: TV series and features. Also stage productions
for cable and PBS. Sonny Fox, pres; Cindy Kunze,
asst to pres. (1978/6)

Franciscan Communications   **(213) 746-2916**
1229 S. Santee St, Los Angeles 90015
F/V/FS/M: materials in the fields of religion, hu-
manity, social conscience. Also print publisher.
Karl Holtsnider producer. (1946/25)

Frankel Films, Inc   **(818) 501-5044**
13418 Ventura Blvd, Sherman Oaks 91423
F: features and TV series. Ernest Frankel, pres.
(1958/2)

John Frankenheimer Productions   **829-0404**
2800 Olympic Blvd. #201, Santa Monica 90404
F: features. John Frankenheimer, producer-dir.

Franklin Film Production Company   **(213) 476-5193**
2460 Roscomare Rd, Los Angeles 90077
F: features. And distribution. (1979/5)

Frankovich Productions   **(213) 278-0920**
9220 Sunset Blvd. #801, Los Angeles 90069
F: features and TV series.

Joel Freeman Productions, Inc   **(818) 995-1189**
3929 Mary Ellen Ave, Studio City 91604
F: features and TV series including Heart Is a
Lonely Hunter, Love at First Bite, etc. (1970)

Fries Entertainment   **(213) 859-9957**
9200 Sunset Blvd, #700, Los Angeles 90069
F: features, TV series, and cable. Charles Fries,
exec producer.

F T G International, Inc   **(213) 467-7210**
1141 Lodi Place, Hollywood 90038
F/V: commercials made in CA mostly for clients in
Japan. Japanese or English. (978/3)

G

GalaVision   **(213) 463-4182**
5358 Melrose Ave, Hollywood 90038
Spanish language cable programing service. Hector
Aculay, creative director.

Galaxy Entertainment Company   **(818) 362-6005**
P O Box 8523, Universal City 91608-0523
Film & TV producer. Dave Gregory, pres; Donald
Ayres, communications. (1979)

Gallerie International Films   **(818) 760-2040**
11320 W. Magnolia, North Hollywood 91601
F: animation & special effects: commercials, TV,
shorts. Distribution, sales, & rental. David Hanson,
pres. (1971/8)

Warren Garfield & Associates (213) 279-1052
6671 Sunset Blvd, Hollywood 90028
F/V: trailers, TV spots; radio spots. Post production facility. Warren Garfield. (1974)

Gaylord Production Company (213) 271-2193
9255 Sunset Blvd. #800, Los Angeles 90069
F/V: features, including Man, Woman, & Child, pilots, syndicated programing. Elmo Williams, exec vp; Jim Terrell, pres; Alan Courtney, pres, television division. (1979/20)

Gaynes Productions Ltd (213) 874-6909 (818) 244-4156
6918 Oporto Drive,Hollywood 90068
Packaging and production of TV series & specials. Lloyd Gaynes, exec prod; Kristen Tellez, prod; Joyce Taylor, writer; Adrienne Lederer, production mgr.

Bo Gehring & Associates 823-8577
13431 Beach Ave, Venice 90292
F: animation & special effects.

Georgian Bay Productions, Ltd (818) 843-7704
3815 W. Olive Ave #101, Burbank CA 91505
F: features. Alex Karras, pres; Susan Clark, vp. (1978/2)

David Gerber Company, Inc (213) 558-6400
10202 W. Washington Blvd, Culver City 90230
F/V: features, including George Washington, miniseries and series, including The Last Days of Pompeii. Fred Whitehead, sen vp; Sandy Climan, vp; Ann Seydor, manager development. (1977/5)

Gilbert American Filmworks (818) 954-6000
4000 Warner Blvd, Burbank 91522
F: features. Bruce Gilbert, prod; Ann Holler, development.

Gileon Associates, Inc (213) 467-1131
5609 Sunset Blvd, Los Angeles 90028
F: features; commercials.

Vern Gillum & Friends, Inc (213) 659-6100
8630 Pinetree Place, Los Angeles 90069
F: commercials. Pat Ludwin, exec producer; Vern Gillum, dir; Morley Skolnek, dir; Sandy Horn, assistant. (1952/7)

Ginsco Productions (213) 855-1453
1204 Corning St, Los Angeles 90035
V/F: B&I; commercials, TV. (1977/4)

Harry Gittes,Inc. (818-985-0430
4225 Coldwater Canyon, Studio City 91604
F: features. Harry Gittes, prod.

Gladden Entertainment Corporation (213) 205-7500
9454 Wilshire Blvd. #309, Beverly Hills 90212
F: features. Bruce McNall, chairman; David Begelman,
pres CEO; Michael Nathanson, pres Motion Picture;
Suzan Waks, vp CFO; Chris Michaels vp business affairs; Ed Morey, vp exec production mgr.

Glass Music Video Productions (213) 666-6546
2811 Waverly Dr #2, Los Angeles 90039
Total music video production from concept to comple-
tion; specializing in new bands. Cinematography
services. Sam Glass, owner/dir of phot.

Global Pictures, Inc (213) 665-5257
4774 Melrose Ave, Los Angeles 90029
F: features. (1968)

G. N. Productions (213) 463-5698
2007 N. Hobart Blvd, Los Angeles 90027
F/V: sports TV programs; commercials, documentaries,
B&I. Gabor Nagy, pres. (1965/5)

Goal Productions, Inc (818) 797-7668
2027 N. Lake Ave, Altadena 91001
F/V: B&I, education, government including the De-
fense Dept. Jack Oswald, pres; John Gura vp; Don
Schroeder, producer, Robert Ballo, production man.
(1970/5)

Steven Gold (213) 467-5177
650 N. Bronson Ave #211, Hollywood 90004
Commercial production; rock videos. Steven Gold,
prod; Helene Bodner, asst prod.

Leonard Goldberg Company (213) 468-4800
5555 Melrose Ave, De Mille Bldg, Hollywood 90038
F: features, including War Games.

Golden Harvest Films, Inc   203-0722
9884 Santa Monica Blvd, Beverly Hills 90212
F: features.

Herb Golden Organization   (818) 985-3300
11331 Ventura Blvd. #303, Studio City 91604
F/V: documentaries and shorts for B&I and education.
Jerry Ross; Ernest Everett, vp. (1961/5)

Golden Image Motion Picture Corp.   (213) 550-8710
9000 Sunset Blvd, #1000, Los Angeles 90069
F: features. Production arm of Intercontinental
Releasing Corporation.

Golden West TV, Inc   (213) 460-5500
5800 Sunset Blvd, Los Angeles 90028
Anthony Cassara, pres CEO. Divisions:

Golden West Entertainment. TV series and specials,
Bill Schickler, vp-general man.

KTLA

Samuel Goldwyn Jr. Company   (213) 552-2255
10203 Santa Moncia Blvd, #500, Los Angeles 90067
F: features including The Golden Seal. Also distribution.

Norman Gollin Productions, Inc   (213) 656-2398
9048 Wonderland Park, Los Angeles 90046
F: B&I. (1961/3)

Goodson-Todman Productions   464-4300
6430 Sunset Blvd, Hollywood 90028
F/V: features, cable, game shows including The Price
Is Right, Tattle Tales, The Family Feud.

Alex Gordon Productions   (213) 936-1874
P O Box 36676, Los Angeles 90036
F: features. Inactive at present.

Lawrence Gordon Productions   (213) 202-2380
3970 Oveland Ave, #207, Culver City 90230
F: features and TV series including Streets of Fire,
Just Our Luck.

Gornick Film Productions   (213) 223-8914
4200 Camino Real, Los Angeles 90065
Film production services; specialty: underwater.
35mm inventory for both sperical and anamorphic
photography. Worldwide experience. Alan Gornick Jr,
pres. (1966)

Bob Graham Productions   (213) 874-7004
1926 Hillcrest Road, Los Angeles 90068
F: features. Also live productions. (1975)

Grand Island Productions   (818) 709-1464
10423 Cozycroft Ave, Chatsworth 91311
TV and motion picture production. Edward Coker,
pres.

Daniel Grant Productions   (213) 935-1022
5725 Calhoun Ave, Van Nuys 91401
F/V: Production budgeting and financing. (978/4)

Sherry Grant Productions   (818) 705-2535
17915 Ventura Bvd. #208, Encino 91316
F/V: entertainment specials (including 21 Days of
America), documentaries, and one-minute documentary
spots with celebrity hosts.   Also syndication.
Sherry Grant, pres; Leslie Anne Van Natta, sales.
(1976/10)

Leonard Grant & Associates, Inc   (213) 274-9483
P O Box 69405, Los Angeles 90069
F: TV specials and features. Night club acts and
personal management. (1961/7)

Graphic Films Corporation   (213) 851-4100
3341 Cahuenga Blvd West, Los Angeles 90068
F: documentaries and B&I and government (JPL &
NASA). Animation, live action, special effects. Also
films in 65mm for Ommnimax-IMAX. (1941/25)

Great American Cinema Company   (213) 475-0937
10711 Wellworth Ave, Los Angeles 90024
F/V: commercials; B&I, education. Casting; post
production facilities; photography services. Glenn
Roland, Jr, dir-exec producer; Claudette Roland,
producer. (1975/5)

The Great American Soap Opera Company (818) 760-8877
11440 Chandler Blvd, #1100, N. Hollywood 91601
F/V: low budget features. Principally distributor.
Richard Damon Aldrich, pres.

Greatheart Productions   (213) 874-0436
982 N. La Brea Ave, Los Angeles 90038
F: features; script writing. Anne Kimmel; Kevin
Hynes; Mark Klein. (1975)

Craig Greene Productions   (213) 874-2305
3518 Cahuenga Blvd West, Los Angeles 90068
F/V: TV programs, features, commercials, B&I. (1979)

Larry Greene Productions   273-0643
1151 Sunset Hills Rd, Los Angeles 90069
Audio for films, records, commercials. Amtek is
subsidiary for radio syndication.

Merv Griffin Productions   (213) 461-4701
1541 N. Vine St, Hollywood 90028
V: TV series including Merv Griffin Show, Jeopardy,
Wheel of Fortune, Dance Fever.

Sherman Grinberg Productions   (213) 464-7491
1040 N. McCadden Place, Los Angeles 90038
Distribution of series. Associated company at same
address: Sherman Grinberg Film Libraries (stock
footage).

Group 1 Films   (213) 550-8767
9200 Sunset Blvd, #1105, Los Angeles 90069
F/V: features, TV series and specials. Distribution
also: domestic and worldwide (The Group 1 International Distributing Organization, Ltd). Brandon
Chase, pres; Marianne Chase, vp; Jack Leff, distribution.

Group Visionary Productions, Inc   (818) 995-6050
13046 Greenleaf St, Studio City 91604
V/F/M: commercials, B&I. Programing Division: net-
work, cable, syndication program development. Larry
Y. Higgs, pres; Barbara Weitz acct. exec; Andee
Nathason, asst. (1971/16)

Group W Cable   829-2676
Regional: 15760 Ventura Blvd, #601, Encino 91436
Operates 15 cable systems in the Los Angeles area
with local offices in each district. Ardie Ivie,
regional director of programing.

Group W Productions   (213) 850-3800
3801 Barham Blvd. #200, Los Angeles 90068
Produces PM Magazine and Hour Magazine.

Michael Gruskoff Productions   (213) 203-3767
PO Box 900, Beverly Hills 90213
F/V: features including Quest for Fire, Until Sep-
tember. (1971/3)

Robert Guenette Productions, Inc   (213) 658-8450
8489 West 3rd St, Los Angeles 90048
F/V: features, TV specials and series. (1976/11)

H

The Haboush Company   (818) 954-6950
3815 W. Olive Ave #102, Burbank 91505
F: commercials. Victor Haboush, dir; Paul Babb,
exec. (1967)

H. B. Halicki Productions   (213) 770-1744
17902 S. Vermont Ave, Gardena 90248
F: action features including Gone in 60 Seconds.
H.B. (Toby) Halicki, owner; Chip Giannettino, director; Dennis Stouffer, marketing. (1974/8)

Paula Lee Haller Productions   (213) 651-0948
8489 W. Third St, Los Angeles 90048
F/V: TV specials including Four Americans in China.
(1979/1)

Handel Film Corporation   (213) 657-8990
8730 Sunset Blvd, Los Angeles 90069
F: B&I, education. Also distribution: sales & rental. Leo Handel, pres. (1953/10)

Bruce Hanifan Productions   **(213) 559-4522**
9046 W. 25th St., Los Angeles 90034
Music and audio production for F/V including sound
design and scoring. Bruce Hanifan, composer, prod;
Jesse Daniels, production mgr. (1979/4)

Hanna-Barbera Productions, Inc   **(213) 851-5000**
3400 Cahuenga Blvd West, Los Angeles 90068
F: animated features, TV series; also live action.
Joseph Barbera, pres; William Hanna, senior vp; Ross
Sutherland, personnel; Ed Pico, administration; Jean
MacCurdy, programing; John Michaeli, communications.
(1957)

Ed Hansen & Associates   **(213) 467-5085**
1454 Seward, Hollywood 90028
F/V: commercials, B&I. Marketing and syndication of
concerts, rock video, and cable TV. Ed Hansen, pres;
Ann Hyatt, production; Robert Gervasoni.

Har Con   **(818) 762-8184**
P O Box 2493, Toluca Lake 91602
F: investigative documentaries, training films,
veteran matters. (1969)

Har D Har Productions, Inc   **(818) 766-5233**
12198 1/2 Ventura Blvd, Studio City 91604
F/V: TV series and features. Gordon Mitchell, pres.
(1972/3)

Larry Harmon Pictures Corporation   **(213) 463-2331**
650 N. Bronson Ave, Los Angeles 90004
F/V: producer, distributor of animated and live
action series: Bozo the Clown; Laurel & Hardy (car-
toon). Larry Harmon, pres; Peter Gerwe, development.
(1958)

Harmony Pictures   **(818) 506-4800**
10623 Riverside Dr, North Hollywood 91602
F: features, commercials, TV, documentaries. Stuart
Gross, producer; Rob Lieberman, dir. (1979)

Harper Conway Productions   **(818) 762-8184**
P O Box 2498, Toluca Lake 91602
F: features. See: Har Con. (1959)

Keith Harrier Production Services   (213) 930-2720
7070 Waring Ave., Los Angeles 90038
Production offices, conference rooms, sound stages, editorial rooms.

Denny Harris Inc of California   (213) 826-6565
12166 Olympic Blvd, Los Angeles 90064
F: commercials. Sound and screening facilities; rental of 16 & 35mm editing equipment. Denny Harris, director; Mary Jo Thatcher, exec producer. (1960)

James B. Harris Productions, Inc   273-4270
248 1/2 S. Lasky Dr, Beverly Hills 90212
F: features including Fast-Walking.

Harris-Tuchman Productions   (818) 841-4100
1226 W. Olive, Burbank 91506
S/FS: primarily health education. Fran Harris, producer. (1950/4)

Hatos-Hall Productions   (213) 874-3000
7833 Sunset Blvd, Los Angeles 90046
V: TV shows including Let's Make a Deal.

Hayden Productions   (213) 879-3257
2029 Century Park East 6th fl, Los Angeles 90067
F/V: features including Exit with Love, TV for cable including Julio Live at the Getty. Gwynne Pineda, pres. (1981)

Headliner Productions   (213) 462-5050
6221 Afton Place, Los Angeles 90028
F: feature (35mm) production, distribution. Roy Reid, pres. (1985)

Helios Productions   (213) 658-5444
8380 Melrose Ave #309, Los Angeles 90069
F: TV features, series, and family specials. Including Contract for Life: The S.A.D.D. Story. Partners: Bradley Wigor, Joseph Maurer; Linda Trescony, associate.

Paul Heller Productions, Inc   (213) 275-4477
1666 N. Beverly Dr, Beverly Hills 90210
F: features including The Promise, First Monday in October, Falcon's Gold. Paul Heller, producer.

Hemdale Leisure Corporation   **(213) 550-6894**
9255 Sunset Blvd, #720, Los Angeles 90069
F: features including Breed Apart.

Heritage Entertainment, Inc   **(213) 278-1566**
9229 Sunset Blvd #414, Los Angeles 90069
F: produces features. Company also develops properties and acquires distribution rights for release to
theatres, TV, payTV, and as video cassette/disc.
Arthur "Skip" Steloff, chairman, pres/dir/prod.;
Samuel Gelfman, vp, development; Robert Steloff,
marketing & acquisitions.

Milan Herzog & Associates, Inc   **(213) 466-8496**
PO Box 206, Hollywood 90028
F/V/FS: shorts. Library of 35mm slides. (1973/3)

Hickmar Productions   **(818) 954-5104**
4000 Warner Blvd, Burbank 91505
F: features. Independent producer of 10 features
including Kidnapped. Marlene Schmidt, prod; Howard
Avedis, prod/dir.

Alfred Higgins Productions, Inc   **(213) 272-6500**
9100 Sunset Blvd, Los Angeles 90069
F/V: educational films. Also distribution. Alfred
Higgins, pres; Audrey Plant, asst to pres; Stephen
Wallen, exec prod. (1958/10)

Hill Production Service   **463-1182**
1139 N. Highland Ave, Hollywood 90038
High speed film cinematography. Video playback for
film cameras and special effects. Jean Hill, pres;
Robert Courtin, manager. (1968/4)

James Hollander & Associates   **(213) 653-1551**
8489 W. Third St, Los Angeles 90048
Post production: film (16 & 35mm); 3/4" videotape.
Specialty is trailers for features. James Hollander,
owner. (1979/3)

Holloway's Eagle Scouts   **(213) 933-9106**
117 La Brea Ave, Los Angeles 90036
Location scouting and management: TV commercials,
features, TV. Still photography. C.R. Holloway,
owner; Ken Titley, 1st assistant; Joe Hosking, 2nd
assistant.

The Hollywood Associates, Inc   **(818) 841-4136**
2800 W. Olive Ave, Burbank 91505
F/V: features, commercials, shorts. Offices in Rome
& London. Michael Carr, pres. (1971) TLX:691-699

Hollywood Film Associates   **(213) 874-8413**
2025 N. Highland Ave, Los Angeles 90068
F/V: features. Production arm of Threshold Films.
Jay Lovins, pres. (1959)

Hollywood Newsreel Syndicate, Inc   **(213) 469-7307**
1622 N. Gower St, Los Angeles 90068
F/V: news & documentary items primarily related to
entertainment industry. Stock footage library: entertainment arts. See: Rick Spalla Video. (1958/4)

Hollywood Theatrical Studios   **(213) 467-8344**
6015 Santa Monica Blvd, Los Angeles 90038
Talent agency. State license nd bonded. Associate
company of Maurice Kosloff Productions.

Home Box Office, Inc (HBO)   **(213) 557-9400**
2049 Century Park East - #4170, Los Angeles 90067
F/V: national Pay TV program service; co-producer of
features and specials. Maurice Singer, vp, film
acquisition; Jane Deknatel, vp, made-for-pay-TV;
Iris Dugow, vp, special programing.

Homer & Associates, Inc   **(213) 462-4710**
1420 N. Beachwood Dr, Hollywood 90028
F/V: music video, home entertainment, and special
programing dir - Peter Conn. Production and post
production optical effects, video editing, computer
painting producer - Coco Conn (1974/5)

Hope Enterprises, Inc   **(818) 841-2020**
3808 Riverside Dr. #100, Burbank 91505
V: produces Bob Hope Specials, other TV specials.

Sandy Howard Productions   **(213) 659-2062**
8833 Sunset Blvd. #301, Los Angeles 90069
F: features including Deadly Force, Angel, Hambone &
Hillie. Keith Rubinstein, exec vp.

IAMC   **(714) 474-2015**
17422 Murphy Ave, Irvine 92714
Recording studio and record pressing. Jerry Shirar, pres. (1976/15)

Image Force   **(213) 458-7995**
9348 Santa Monica Blvd #101, Beverly Hills 90210
F: documentaries; coordination of other film/video projects. Specialty is to assist American production companies wishing to sell in the Japanese market; or wish to shoot in Japan. Shinjiro Kanazawa, pres, exec prod; Lucy Seligman, vp prod. (1979/5)

IndieProd Company   **(818) 954-2600**
4000 Warner Blvd. Prod Bldg 7-1, Burbank 91505
F: features including Altered States. Daniel Melnick, pres-producer.

Ingels Inc.   **(213) 852-0300**
8322 Beverly Blvd. #207, Los Angeles 90048
Puts the star-buyers in touch with the celebrities: for commercials, TV series, features, shorts, benefits, personal appearances, radio, press. Larry Crane, pres. (1976/22)

Innovation Unlimited   **(213) 823-4251**
4444 Via Marina (Penthouse 81), Marina del Rey 90292
F/V: commercials, B&I. Program development for syndication, network, cable. Post production facility. Rand Rubin, CEO. (1972/4)

I/O Productions, Inc   **(213) 655-4201**
8480 W. Beverly Blvd, Los Angeles 90048
V: documentaries, B&I, shorts, and news pieces for European and American TV. Producers of Musicalifornia (on French TV). Equipment rental. Claude Gaignare, pres. (1983/5)

Instruct. Systems for Health Sciences (213) 477-8541
11899 W. Pico Blvd, West Los Angeles 90064
F/V/S/FS/audio cassettes: production and distribution primarily in health field. Dr. Richard Boolootian, pres; Mary Jo Blue, production. (1968/4)

Intercontinental Releasing Corp.   **(213) 550-8710**
9000 Sunset Blvd #1000, Los Angeles 90069
F/V: feature; and worldwide distribution. Sandy
Cobe, pres; Alex Rebar, project development; Greg
Ferguson, vp production. (1970/11)

International Medifilms   **(213) 851-4555**
3393 Barham Blvd, Los Angeles 90068
F: primarily medicine, and health related subjects
for business. Distribution (sales and rental).
Gerald Price, pres. (1970/15)

International TV Film Productions   **(818) 888-2277**
5850 Canoga Ave #110, Woodland Hills 91267
F: features and TV specials. (1972/2)

Inter-Ocean Film Sales, Inc   **(21) 557-1400**
9000 Sunset Blvd #615, Los Angeles 90069
F: features. Finance and foreign distribution. Associated company: Film Packages International.
(1969/4)

Inter Planetary Productions Corp   **(818) 981-4950**
14225 Ventura Blvd, Sherman Oaks 91423
F/V: features including Kent State. International
distribution through Inter Planetary Pictures, Inc.
Max Keller, chairman; Micheline H. Keller, pres;
Patricia Herskovic, exec vp. (1976/15)

Interscope Communications, Inc   **(213) 208-8525**
10900 Wilshire Blvd. #1400, Los Angeles 90024
F/V: features including Revenge of the Nerds; development and production. TV and cable programing.
Frederick W. Field, pres parent company; Robert
Cort, pres, Entertainment Division; Peter Samuelson
vp development-production. (1977/10)

Intralink Film Graphic Design   **(213) 859-7001**
155 N. Lapeer Dr, Los Angeles 90048
Print & A/V design communication group. Anthony
Goldschmidt, pres; Marc Gerber, prod.; John Alvin,
creative director.

Introvision Systems   **(213) 851-9262**
1011 N. Fuller, Hollywood 90046
Motion picture production/special effects. (1980/10)

Iota Productions   **(213) 652-3223**
1220 Sunset Plaza Dr, Los Angeles 90069
F: features and B&I. Kelly Ross & Gabriel E.
Gyorffy. (1967)

ITC Productions, Inc   **(818) 760-2110**
12711 Ventura Blvd, Studio City 91604
F: features including Sophie's Choice, The Evil That
Men Do. Jerry Leider, pres; Dennis Brown, exec in
charge of production; Arthur Kananack, exec in
charge of business.

J

Jacobs & Gerber, Inc   **(213) 655-4082**
731 N. Fairfax Ave, Los Angeles 90046
F/V: commercials. Full advertising agency, specializing in broadcast promotion. (1974)

David Jackson Productions   **(714) 594-6344**
19600 Lencho Place, Walnut 91789
Creative film and TV productions of human interest
stories.

Michael Jacobs   **(818) 508-3117**
100 Universal Plaza, Universal City 91608
TV producer/writer (Charles In Charge, No Soap Radio); Playwright (Gettling Along Famously).

Jaffe-Lansing Productions   **(213) 468-4575**
5555 Melrose Ave, Los Angeles 90038
Independent motion picture producer. Partners:
Sherry Lansing, Stanley Jaffe; Susan Merzbach vp.

Henry Jaffe Enterprises, Inc   **(213) 466-3543**
1420 N. Beachwood Dr, Los Angeles 90028
F/V: TV series and features. Subsidiary interest in
music publishing, recordings, and live theatre.
(1954/8)

Jaguar Productions, Inc   (213) 653-7553
8052 Melrose Ave, Los Angeles 90046
F: commercials. NY office. Ron Jacobs, dir; Shirley
Dieu, office manager. (1972/15)

Jeffries Films International   (818) 760-6666
3855 Lankershim Blvd, North Nollywood CA 91604
F: commercials. Hugh Jeffries, exec producer; Jim
O'Neil, director. (1975/10)

Jenner/Wallach Productions   (213) 278-4574
1400 Braeridge Dr, Beverly Hills 90210
Film production. George Wallach, Bruce Jenner.

Mark Jerod Productions   (818) 989-2726
17073 Mooncrest Dr, Encino 91316
F/V: commercials. Theatrical and TV development.
Stanley M. Lazan, owner.

Jewish TV Network   (213) 614-0972
617 S. Olive St, #515, Los Angeles 90014
Cable program service.

Norman Jewison See: Yorktown Productions   202-3402

JJH Productions Inc   (213) 682-3611 682-2353
900 Palm Ave, South Pasadena 91030
F/V: complete video and film (16 & 35mm) production:
industrial, educational, commercial, thetrical. Gay
Hennessy, COO, prod; Greg Bonann, development; Steve
Kovner, production coordinator.

Joda Productions   (213) 652-6263
1437 Rising Glen Rd, Los Angeles 90069
Motion picture production; development, scripting,
and packaging. David Sheldon, pres/prod/writer; Joan
McCall, vp, writer/prod.

Johnson/Cowan Inc   (213) 466-5301
1601 N. El Centro Ave, Los Angeles 90028
F/V: commercials. (1971/14)

Kenneth Johnson Productions, Inc   (818) 905-5255
4528 Colbath Ave. #8, Sherman Oaks 91423
F: TV programs including Shadow Chasers.

Johnson Nyquist Productions, Inc   **(714) 770-5777**
23854 Via Fabricante - #D1, Mission Viejo 92691
F/V: commercials, shorts. David Johnson, Carroll
Nyquist. (1967/7)

Joyce Media,   **(805) 269-1169**
P O Box 57, Acton 93510
F/V: films for deaf or hearing impaired people.
Principal business is publishing for same audience.
John Joyce, pres. (1973/10)

Jozak Company   **(213) 653-1592**
7469 Melrose Ave #28, Los Angeles 90046
F: features and TV series. Gerald I. Isenberg, pres.
(1973/4)

JSK Enterprises, Inc   **553-1525**
470 S. Bedford Dr, Beverly Hills 90212
F: features including The Final Terror. (1978)

Juno Productions, Inc   **(213) 201-2300**
1875 Cenutry Park East #700, Los Angeles 90067
F: features (1979)

K

KABC-TV   **(213) 557-7777**
4151 Prospect Ave, Hollywood 90027
Channel 7 (ABC). Thomas K. Van Amburg, vp, general
manager.

Kaleidoscope Films, Ltd   **(213) 465-1151**
844 N. Seward St, Los Angeles 90038
F/V: motion picture trailers, featurettes, TV and
radio spots. Post production facility. Andrew J.
Kuehn, pres. (1965/40)

Kaleidoscope Film & Tape, Inc   **(213) 465-6802**
844 N. Seward St, Los Angeles 90038
F: commercials, documentaries, shorts. David Stoltz,
exec prod; Stephen Netburn, prod; Vincent Arcaro
production mgr.

Leonard Katzman　　　　　　　　**(213) 202-4215**
3970 Overland Ave, Culver City 90230
F: TV series including Dallas. (1970)

Kavich/Reynolds Productions　　　**(213) 466-2490**
6381 Hollywood Blvd #580, Hollywood 90028
F/V: B&I; new product/service introduction; employee
orientations etc. John Reynolds, prod; Steve Kavich,
prod; Doug Henry, dir.

William Kayden Productions　(213) 312-4803 271-5903
999 N. Doheny Dr #309, Los Angeles 90069
TV and motion picture production. William Kayden,
pres.; Matthew Kayden, development.

KCBS　　　　　　　　　　　　**(213) 460-3000**
6121 Sunset Blvd, Hollywood 90028
Channel 2 (CBS). Frank Gardiner, vp, general mgr.

KCET　　　　　　　　　　　　**(213) 666-6500**
4401 Sunset Blvd, Los Angeles 90027
Channel 28 (PBS). William H. Kobin, pres; Donald G.
Youpa, sen vp, development-marketing.

KCOP-TV　　　　　　　　　　**(213) 851-1000**
915 N. La Brea Ave, Hollywood 90038
Channel 13. Bill Frank, president.

Stacy Keach Prod　　(213) 877-0472 (818) 762-0966
5216 Laurel Canyon Blvd, North Hollywod 91607
F/V: B&I, commercials. Multi-media and live presentations for business and organizations. (1946/8)

KHJ-TV　　　　　　　　　　　**(213) 462-2133**
5515 Melrose Ave, Hollywood 90038
Channel 9. Charles Velona, vp, general manager.

King International Corporation　　**(213) 274-0333**
124 Lasky Dr, Beverly Hills 90212
F: features and TV series. Principal business is
hotels. Frank King, pres; Herman King, vp.

King Videocable Company　　　**(818) 352-4447**
10000 Commerce Ave, Tujuna 91042
Cable franchise with access channels. Morrie Prizer,
system manager.

Kings Road Productions   (213) 552-0057
1901 Avenue of the Stars #605, Los Angeles 90067
F: features including Best of Times, Creator.
Stephen Friedman, chairman, prod; Clive Parsons,
pres. (1974)

KLCS-TV   (213) 625-6958
1061 W Temple, Los Angeles 90012
Channel 58. Station of the Los Aneles Unified School
District. Tom Mossman, station manager; Patricia
Marshall, educational programing.

Klein &   (213) 278-5600
1111 S. Robertson Blvd, Los Angeles 90035
F/V: broadcasting-cable promotions; commercials.
Animation design; music; consultation; cable program
development. Bob Klein, pres; Barbara Abels, marketing; Jill Green, creative services; Bruce
Littlejohn, production. (1960/20)

Robert D. Kline (Trans-Atlantic Enterprises) 454-6515
101 Ocean Ave, Santa Monica 90402
F/V: documentaries, TV series, features. (1975/3)

KMEX-TV   (213) 466-8131
5420 Melrose Ave, Los Angeles 90038
Channel 34. Spanish language. Sandra Gibson, station
manager.

KNBC   (818) 840-4444
3000 W. Alameda Ave, Burbank 91523
Channel 4 (NBC). John Rohrbeck, vp, gen manager.

Howard W. Koch   (213) 468-5996
5555 Melrose Ave, Los Angeles 90038
F: features.

Korean Television Productions   (213) 935-1289
5225 Wilshire Blvd. #420, Los Angeles 90036
V: commercials and shorts. KWHY-TV channel 22 is the
broadcasting arm. (1971/4)

Maurice Kosloff Productions   (213) 466-4245
6015 Santa Monica Blvd, Los Angeles 90038
F: features (1935). Maurice Kosloff, exec prod;
Michael Lipman, associate.

Kragen Productions, Inc (213) 854-4400
1112 N. Sherbourne Dr, Los Angeles 90069
F/V: features and mini-series including Gambler II.
Also personal management. Ken Kragen, producer;
Kenneth Yates, vp COO. (1979/3)

Jerry Kramer & Associates, Inc (213) 462-2680
1312 N. La Brea Ave, Hollywood 90028
F/V: commercials, motion picture trailers and promotions, B&I, music video. Specialty is special effects and computer animation. Post production facilities: film & tape. Jerry Kramer, pres. (1977/13)

KSCI (213) 479-8081
1950 Cotner Ave, Los Angeles 90025
Channel 18. Tom Headly, gen manager. See: Chinese
World Television.

KTLA 460-5500
5800 Sunset Blvd PO Box 500, Hollywood 90028
Channel 5. Golden West Television. Steven A. Bell,
senior vp, general manager.

KTTV (213) 462-7111
5746 Sunset Blvd, Hollywood 90028
Channel 11. Metromedia. Bill White, vp general mgr.

Kurtz & Friends Films (818) 841-8188
2312 W. Olive Ave, Burbank 91506
F: animation studio. Commercials, special effects,
special projects. (1974/20)

L

L/A House Productions (213) 216-5813
5822 Uplander Way, Culver City 90230
F/V: shorts, features. Writing consultants. Kenneth
Atchity, pres; John Graves, vp. (1977/7)

N Lee Lacy/Associates, Ltd   **(213) 852-1414**
8446 Melrose Place, Los Angeles 90069
F: commercials, features, cable TV. Offices in NY,
Chicago, London, Paris, Germany. Benson Green, pres;
N. Lee Lacy, chairman; David Tate, exec producer;
Chris Mortensen, exec producer. (1962/40)

The Ladd Company   **(213) 954-4400**
4000 Warner Blvd, Burbank 91522
F: features. (1979)

Laird International Studios   **(213) 836-5537**
9336 W. Washington Blvd, Culver City 90230
Studio includes 12 sound stages, sound facility,
company offices. Airplane mockups. Jack Kindberg,
general manager; Linda Hart, studio coordinator.

Laissez-Faire Films   **(213) 938-1567**
937 N Cole #6, Los Angeles 90038
F: commercials, B&I. Ross Kelsay, dir; Carol Kelsay,
exec prod; Stanley Gaissforth, sales. (1978)

Lajon Productions, Inc   **(818) 841-1440**
2907 W. Olive Ave, Burbank 91505
F: features, commercials, B&I. Lawrence Applebaum,
pres; Edward Lapple, general man; Harvey Genkins,
creative vp. (1974/7)

LaLoggia Productions, Inc   **(213) 462-3055**
2700 Rinconia, Los Angeles 90028
F: features including Fear No Evil. Frank LaLoggia,
dir-producer.

Edie & Ely Landau, Inc   **(213) 553-5010**
2029 Century Park East (#460), Los Angeles 90067
F/V: features and cable, including Separate Tables
(HBO).

Landfall Productions, Inc   **(213) 461-5462**
2022 1/2 N. Argyle Ave, Los Angeles 90068
F: features. Development & productions. (1977)

The Landsburg Company   **(213) 208-2111**
11811 W. Olympic Blvd, Los Angeles 90064
F/V: features and TV series, including Give Me a
Break. Alan Landsburg. (1971)

Walter Lantz Productions, Inc   **(213) 469-2907**
6311 Romaine St, Hollywood 90038
F: animation studio. (1920)

The Larry Larry Company   **(818) 954-2526**
Columbia Pictures Television, Burbank 91505
F/V: TV series. Larry Rosen & Larry Tucker, exec
producers.

Bob Larsen Productions   **(818) 501-5533**
16055 Ventura Blvd. #700, Encino 91436
F: B&I, TV series. Dr. Jerry Fecht, dir marketing.

Las Palmas Productions   **(213) 467-5222**
1138 n. Las Palmas, Hollywood 90038
Live action, special effects. William Barnett, vp,
gen manager.

Ben Lautman Productions   **(213) 467-2116**
4736 Admiralty Way #11416, Marina del Rey 90295

Suzanne & Bernard Lax   **(213) 550-4550**
9105 Carmelita Ave, #1, Beverly Hills 90210
F: features, TV specials. Also talent management.
Also known as: LAX International FilmWorks. (1970)

Jerry Leider Productions   **(818) 760-2110**
12711 Ventura Blvd, Studio City 91604
Production in abeyance; Mr. Leider president of ITC
Productions.

Malcolm Leo Productions   **(213) 464-4448**
6536 Sunset Blvd, Hollywood 90028
F: features, variety specials including ET and
Friends.

Leonard Films, Inc   **(818) 783-0457**
5300 Fulton Ave, Van Nuys 91401
F: features. Herbert B. Leonard, pres-prod. (1966)

J. K. Lesser Productions   **(213) 466-8149**
5319 Hollywood Blvd, Los Angeles 90027
B&I marketing sound/slides & videocassettes.
(1961/7)

Levinson Entertainment Ventures Int. (213) 460-4545
650 N. Bronson Ave #250, Los Angeles 90004
Packaging and production of motion pictures and TV.
Robert S. Levinson, pres; Sandra Levinson vp production; Alison Chez, production asst.

Levy-Gardner-Laven Productions (213) 278-9820
9570 Wilshire Blvd. #400, Beverly Hills 90212
F: features including Gator. Jules Levy, pres;
Arthur Gardner, vp; Arnold Laven, vp. (1951/5)

Mort Libov Productions, Inc (213) 469-3111
1438 N. Gower (#550), Los Angeles 90028
F/V: commercials, TV programing, music video. (1970)

Harry Liles Productions (213) 466-1612
1060 N. Lillian Way, Los Angeles 90038
F/V: commercials. Also advertising photography.
(1973)

Lima Productions (213) 464-2220
723 N Cahuenga Blvd, Hollywood 90088
F: features including Summer School.

Richard O. Linke Associates (818) 760-2500
4445 Cartwright Ave #110, North Hollywood 91602
Personal manager and TV producer.

Lion's Gate Films (213) 820-7751
1861 S. Bundy Dr, Los Angeles 90025
F: features including Under Fire. Jonathan Taplin,
pres.

Little Sister Pictures, Inc (213) 850-0473
1958 Glencoe Way, Hollywood 90068
F/V: production for the consumer. Videocassettes:
education, health, B&I. Rupert Macnee, producer;
Heather Stewart, production manager. (1979/3)

Livingston/5 (213) 851-5051
1516 N. Formosa Ave, Los Angeles 90046
F/V: commercials. Creative advertising. Lee
Livingston, dir; Dan Martin, prod; Linda Gordon,
sales; Marilyn Penn, production mgr. (1978/5)

Lone Star Pictures International (213) 463-3175
1347 N. Cahuenga Blvd, Hollywood 90028
F: features. And distribution.

Lori Productions   **(213) 466-7567**
6430 Sunset Blvd. #1217, Los Angeles 90028
F/M: B&I, corporate communications, educational news
releases. Also live presentations. Jack Wipper,
pres; William Hilliard, vp project development;
Charity Carlson, A/V services. (1961/5)

Lorimar Productions   **(213) 202-2000**
3970 Overland Ave, Culver City 90230
F: produces features including Tank, and TV series
(Dallas, Falcon Crest, Knot's Landing, Our Family
Honor, Bridges to Cross, Valerie). Lee Rich, pres.
Development: Joanne Brough, vp-creative affairs;
Jeff Benson, exec vp-TV; Madeline Warren, vp-fea-
tures.

Edward J. Lund   **(213) 851-0754**
3208 Cahuenga Blvd West #13, Los Angeles 90068
F/V: features, TV series on cable including Aware
Magazine. (1983/4)

A. C. Lyles Productions   **(213) 468-5000**
5555 Melrose Ave, Hollywood 90038
Motion picture and TV production company; TV series
and specials. A.C. Lyles, exec prod; Mary-Ann
Dunlap, asst to prod.

M

MacGillivray-Freeman Films   **(714) 494-1055**
P O Box 205, South Laguna 92677
F: specialty shooting for commercials, features,
B&I. Producer-photographer of IMAX film (To Fly).
(1966/6)

Lee Madden Associates   **(213) 459-5198**
16918 Marquez Ave, Pacific Palisades 90272
Motion pictures, theatricals, TV, & commercials. Lee
Madden, pres.

Douglas Mador Productions   **(213) 651-1278**
804 N. Sierra Bonita Ave, Los Angeles 90046
F/V: features and TV specials, series. (1951)

Malpaso Productions   **(818) 954-6000**
4000 Warner Blvd, Burbank 91522
F: features. Clint Eastwood, producer; Fritz Manes, prod; David Valdes, assoc prod.

Ted Mann Productions, Inc   **(213) 273-3336**
9200 Sunset Blvd. #200, Los Angeles 90069
F: features including Krull. Ted Mann, pres; Ron Silverman, producer. (1967)

Mann & Goldstein   **(213) 467-4520**
7046 Hollywood Blvd. #409, Los Angeles 90028
F: features, commercials, educational shorts, TV series for cable. Allan Mann, pres; Rebecca Goldstein, vp. (1978/2)

Manson International   **(213) 208-8899**
11355 Olympic Blvd, Los Angeles 90064
F:features. International distributor: Manson Video (video cassette) and Manson Cable. Michael Goldman, pres; Peter Elson vp-acquis. (1953) TLX 691 242

Marchak Productions   **(213) 461-3200**
1041 N. Mansfield Ave, Hollywood CA 90038
F/V: commercials, promotions, show segments. Film style video a specialty. Patrick Marty, pres. (1979/5)

Marcom Productions, Inc   **(213) 820-6867**
12150 W. Olympic Blvd, Los Angeles 90064
F/V/S/M: B&I; music shows for cable. (1970/5)

Marjon Presentations   **(818) 994-2098**
7534 Woodley Ave, Van Nuys 91406
F/V/FS: shorts on values, lifestyles, and management. Also dramatic shorts to cable and theatrical market. S. Marc Tapper & Karl Kempwolf, producers; Aicda Jiccardi, production coordinator. (1974/3)

Market Street Productions   **(213) 396-5937**
73 Market St, Venice 90291
F: features: Tony Bill, prod-dir. Production, post production facilities available: Ellen Morbetske, manager.

Markowitz/Chesler Producing Corp.   **(213) 461-7825**
6565 Sunset Blvd #400, Hollywood 90028
V: total production. See Cabala Communications.

Marks Communications   **(213) 936-3464**
5550 Wilshire Blvd #306, Los Angeles 90036
High level computer animation, design for broadcast.
Harry Marks, creative dir; Vance Martin, prod.

Thomas L. Marshall Productions, Inc   **(818) 700-8235**
PO Box 155, Beverly Hills 90213
F: features including The Glory of Khan. J.H. Hanen,
pres; T.L. Marshall, vp.

Marstar Productions   **(818) 508-2095**
100 Universal City Plaza, Universal City 91608
F; features. Also produces projects for legitimate
stage. Martin Starger, pres; Howard Alston, vp;
Dennis Doty, TV exec; Ginny Durkin, exec asst to
pres.

Jill Marti Productions   **(213) 463-2166**
650 N. Bronson, Los Angeles 90004
F/V: TV movies (The Shadow Box) & Cable variety
series. Jill Marti; Drew Suss. (1977)

Ed Marzola & Associates   **(818) 506-7788**
11846 Ventura Blvd, Studio City 91604
F/V: features, specials (including World Cup Soccer
- Mexico 86), commercials. Offices in five coun-
tries. Bill Case vp; D. O'Neil, manager. (1968/5)

Masai Enterprises, Inc   **(213) 466-5451**
6922 Hollywood Blvd. #401, Hollywood 90028
F/V: commercials, documentaries, shorts, features.
All formats film and tape shooting editing. Fritz
Goode, producer-dir; Denise Nicholas, producer, Joe
Wilcots, producer-cinematographer. (1974/8)

Gene Massey Films   **(213) 476-3668**
550 S. Barrington Ave. #2209, Los Angeles 90049
F: comedy & fantasy-oriented B&I; commercials.
(1979/3)

Maynor Enterprises   **(213) 277-5881**
P O Box 1641, Beverly Hills 90212
F/V: features including The Wicked Stepmother. Asa
Maynor, exec producer. (1977)

Max Films   **(213) 662-3285**
2525 Hyperion Ave, Los Angeles 90027
F/V: B&I, educat. Kel Christiansen, pres. (1970/6)

Paul Mazursky   (818) 840-1000
Disney Studio, 500 S. Buena Vista St, Burbank 91521
F: features including Tempest.

Eugene Mazzola Enterprises, Inc   (213) 851-8750
14475 156th NE, Woodinville WA 98072 (206) 483-8840
F:features and commercials. Production management
service. (1975)

MCA-TV   (818) 985-4321
100 Universal City Plaza, Universal City 91608
Distributor of TV programing. Division of MCA, Inc.

Gene McCabe Productions   (818) 841-2030
140 E Providencia, Burbank 91503
TV and motion picture production. Gene McCabe, owner.

Meadowlane Enterprises, Inc   (818) 988-3830
15201 Burbank Blvd. #B, Van Nuys 91411
Office of Steve Allen. Production through other
companies.

Laszlo Mecs Films   (213) 465-8290
1140 N. Beachwood Dr. #D, Hollywood 90038
F: commercials, features, documentaries, B&I.
(1975/5)

Medallion TV Enterprises, Inc   (213) 652-8100
8831 Sunset Blvd, West Hollywood 90069
F: TV series and features. Principally distributor.
(1955/5)   TWX-910-490-1139

Media Four Productions   (818) 848-5552
724 S. Victory Blvd, Burbank 91502
F/V: B&I programs. Extensive experience in technical
and scientific subjects. Charles Finance. (1973/1)

Media Learning Systems, Inc   (818) 449-0006
1532 Rose Villa St, Pasadena 91106
F/V: B&I. Specialist in interactive videodisc design, production, and systems integration. James F.
Griffith, pres; Mitch Aiken, production mgr.
(1977/8)

Media Group, Ltd (MGL)   (818) 506-7227
11846 Ventura Blvd 2nd fl, Studio City 91604
See: Armstrong Creative Services.

The Media & Talent Organization (MTO) (213) 271-4629
P O Box 2310, Beverly Hills 90213-2310
Film/TV producer: features, docudramas, documentaries, education & industrial A/V programs. Consultants to communication, industry, education, media. Specializes in international production/co-production. Affiliated offices in Europe & Latin America. Eric Heckscher, pres. (1953/28)

Mediators Productions (213) 456-2512
20269 Inland Lane, Malibu 90265
The company develops and promotes products for the electronic media in which characters deal with reducing the risk of nuclear war, seeking nonviolent alternatives, and raising children in a threatening world. Mark Gerzon, pres.

Medigraphics, Inc (213) 463-1644
1626 N Wilcox #315, Hollywood 90028
F/V: medical/pharmaceutical films. Extensive TV documentary credits for scientific, medical, technical subjects. Mike O'Rourke, pres. (1977/4)

Bill Melendez Productions, Inc (213) 463-4101
439 N. Larchmont Blvd, Los Angeles 90004
F: animation studio; TV series (including Charley Brown), features, commercials. (1964/30)

Mercury Entertainment Corporation (213) 557-7463
2020 Ave of the Stars, Los Angeles 90067
Independent film production company. Successor by merger to Michael Phillips Productions (credits include The Sting, Close Encounters of the Third Kind, The Flamingo Kid).

Mesa Film Productions (213) 464-8381
P O Box 8896, Universal City 91608
F: features, especailly low budget exploitation films including Malibu Hot Summer and Georgis County Lockup. Co-production invited. Eric Louzil, pres; Laurel Koernig, vp. (1977/10).

META-4 Productions, Inc (213) 654-6686
8300 Santa Monica Blvd. #203, Los Angeles 90069
F/V: documentaries, TV series, commercials, B&I. Terry Carter, president.

Burt Metcalfe   **(213) 203-2365**
10201 W. Pico Blvd, Los Angeles 90035
F: executive producer of TV series including After-
MASH.

Metro-Goldwyn-Mayer Film Company   **(213) 558-5000**
10202 W. Washington Blvd, Culver City 90230
F:features.

Metromedia Producers Corporation   **(213) 462-7111**
5746 Sunset Blvd, Hollywood 90028
F/V: features, TV series for syndication, network,
and cable. Charles D. Young, pres; Ethel Vinant, sen
vp-creative affairs; Chet Collier, exec vp-distribu-
tion; Dale Sheets, vp-production.

MFI (Manny's Filmakers, Inc)   **(213) 851-0373**
1905 Grace Ave, Hollywood 90068
F/V: commercials, features, B&I, music video. Film
to tape transfer. Manuel S. Conde, pres. (1968/3)

MGM-UA Entertainment Co.   **(213) 558-5000**
10202 W. Washington Blvd, Culver City 90230
Alan Ladd, Jr, pres., CEO. Parent company of MGM
Film Co, United Artists Corp, and MGM/UA-TV.

MGM-UA TV
Larry Gershman, pres, worldwide distribution
MGM/UA Television Broadcast Group
David Grober, pres, worldwide production. Lynn
Loring, sen vp, programing & production. Develop-
ment: Diana Dreiman, vp, comedy; Tony Jonas, vp,
drama, series, movies, miniseries. TV series in-
clude: Fame, Kids Incorporated, Lady Blue.

Michael/Daniel Productions   **(213) 464-7307**
7025 Santa Monica Blvd, Hollywood 90038
F: commercials. Michael Romersa, Dan Nichols.
(1979/10)

Mileham Entertainment Inc   **(213) 464-7116**
2441 N. Beachwood Ave #2, Hollywood 90046
Feature film, documentary, and music video production. Michael Mileham, director; Marily Ellis, music
supervisor.

Edward Milkis Productions   **(213) 468-5901**
5555 Melrose Ave, Hollywood 90038

Deke Miles & Associates   (213) 466-2825
6123 Glen Oak, Los Angeles 90068
F: commercials, features. Associated with Cactus
Tree Productions.

Warren Miller Enterprises Inc   (213) 376-2494
P O Box 536, Hermosa Beach 90254
F/V: sports cinematography; innovators in filmed
sports, including Sky Country. Full production facilities plus distribution/bartering. Sports stock
footage library. Warren Miller, pres; Don Brohn,
production mgr; Kurt Miller, Sim Hinds, marketing.

Mirage Product. See: Sydney Pollack   (818) 954-1711

The Mirisch Corporation   (818) 985-4321
100 Universal City Plaza, Universal City 91608
F: features including Romantic Comedy. Walter
Mirisch.

Mitam Productions   (818) 987-3478
1607 North El Centro #3, Los Angeles 90028
Motion picture production and distribution. Wes
DePue, pres.

MKD Productions   (213) 654-8070
8230 Beverly Blvd #17, Los Angeles 90048
Company produces a variety of programing for TV and
film. Muffett Kaufman, pres; Douglas Ross, associate.

MMA, Inc   (213) 852-1956
8484 Wilshire Blvd. #235, Beverly Hills 90211
F; features. Aaron Schwab, pres; Faye Schwab, vp.
(1982)

Moctesuma Esparza Productions   (213) 269-8251
912 N. Eastern Ave, Los Angeles 90063
F: commercials, B&I, features, documentaries. Bilin-
gual (Spanish). Karen F. Ochoa, production. (1947/7)

Moffitt-Lee Productions   (213) 557-4052
1438 N Gower, Los Angeles 90028
V: TV series Fridays, Not Necessarily News. John
Moffitt, prod; Pat Lee co prod. (1979/40)

Morgan-Hillinger Films (213) 532-1306
216 36th Place, Manhattan Beach 90266
Distribution: foreign theatrical; domestic cable.
Kathy Morgan, distribution; Brad Hillinger, production. (1978/3)

Morse Entertainment Grp(213) 276-9021 (818) 786-3114
205 S. Beverly Dr #206, Beverly Hills 90212
Personal management, TV production. Adam Sandler, pres; Eric Ige, vp, bus. affairs; Mark Adams, dir. creative affairs.

Motion Picture Marine, Inc (213) 822-1100
616 Venice Blvd, Marina del Rey 90291
F/V: features, commercials, documentaries, B&I. Specialty is on the water and underwater production. Camera boat and marine equipment and crew. David Grober, pres-producer; Douglas Merrifield, producer. (1977/6)

Motion Picture Photography (213) 462-4266
6363 Sunset Blvd #826, Hollywood CA 90028
Mailing address: PO Box 1859, Los Angeles 90078
V: production & services: commercials, TV pilots. Mr. Elia Ravasz, owner/director.

Motionpicture Recording, Inc (213) 462-6897
7060 Hollywood Blvd, Hollywood 90028
Audio post production house. Scoring stage. 35mm dubbing stage. Garry Ulmer, pres; Bernice Moschini, studio mgr. (1970)

Motivational Media, Inc (213) 465-3194
6855 Santa Monica Blvd, Los Angeles 90038
Distributor of educational material. See: Avanti Films. (1965/8)

Motown Productions (213) 461-9954
6255 Sunset Blvd, Hollywood 90028
F/V: features, including Happy Endings, TV series and specials, including Motown Returns to the Apollo. Stage Productions. (1970)

The Movie Machine, Inc (213) 273-3838
838 N Doheny Dr #904, Los Angeles 90069
F: features including Skatetown U.S.A. William Levey, pres. (1975/2)

MTM   **(818) 760-5000**
4024 Radford Ave, Studio City 91604
F/V: TV series and features, including Hill Street
Blues, Newhart, Remington Steele. Arthur Price,
pres; Stuart Erwin Jr, exec vp-creative affairs; Tom
Parry, vp motion pictures; John Scheinfeld, vp development.

Multi-Media-Works   **(213) 939-1185**
7227 Beverly Blvd, Los Angeles 90036
M/S/F/V productions. Video animatics from story-
boards. Art GaNung. (1966/3)

Murakami/Wolf/Swenson Films, Inc   **(213) 462-6474**
1463 Tamarind Ave, Hollywood 90028
F: TV series, features (including The Magic Egg),
commercials. Specialty: animation over live action.
Fred Wolf, director. (1963/12)

Jack Murphy Associates   **(818) 766-4330**
12746 Tiara St, N. Hollywood 91607
V: sports telecasts for U.S. and via satellite for
multidestinational international viewers. Expert in
teleconferencing. (1971)

Mike Murphy Productions   **(213) 655-4879**
6363 Wilshire Blvd, #228, Los Angeles 90048
F: features, documentaries, TV series. Mike Murphy,
producer. (1978/6)

N

Gary Nardino Productions   **(213) 468-5770**
5555 Melrose Ave, Los Angeles 90038
Motion picture and TV production. Gary Nardino,
pres; Chip Hayes vp; Susan Zachary, development.

Nason Media   **(714) 978-8112**
Suite 115, 2040 S. Santa Cruz, Anaheim 92805
V: religious programing. TV series, commercials.
Producer of Robert Schuller's Hour of Power. Michael
Nason, pres. (1974/25)

National Educational Media, Inc   **(818) 709-6009**
Suite 300, 21601 Devonshire St, Chatsworth 91311
F/V: Educational, B&I shorts. Principally a distri-
butor.

National Telefilm Associates, Inc   **(213) 306-4040**
12636 Beatrice St, Los Angeles 90066
Distributor: TV series and features. Bud Groskopf,
pres; Arthur Gross, world sales. (1951/30)

National Television News, Inc   **(818) 883-6121**
23480 Park Sorrento #213A
F/V: B&I, financial subjects; TV news, PSA. Howard
Back, pres; Jim O'Donnell, vp. (1960/9)

NBC Entertainment   **(818) 840-4444**
3000 W. Alameda Ave, Burbank 91523
National Broadcasting Company. Grant Tinker, chairman & CEO, Brant Tartikoff, president.
TV series include Punky Brewster. (Bill Cosby Show
produced in NY by Casey-Werner Productions.)
Charles Goldstein vp, feature & mini-series production.

N.B.I. Filmworks Inc   **(213) 859-1921 (213) 822-0847**
400 S. Beverly Drive #214, Beverly Hills 90212
TV commercials, music videos, TV shows. Still photography. Noby Noda, dir/prod.

Neila Productions   **(213) 876-7826**
1410 N. Curson Ave, Hollywood CA 90046
F/V: features and TV programing. Stanley Ralph Ross,
vp. (1974)

The Nelson Company   **(818) 873-2431**
5400 Shirley Ave, Tarzana 91356
F/V/FS: B&I. Also live theatre production. Philip
Abbott, pres. (1970/3)

New World Pictures, Inc   **(213) 551-1444**
1888 Century Park East (5h Fl), Los Angeles 90067
F: features. Also distribution.

Newby's Movies   **(818) 763-5878**
6026 Wilkinson Ave, North Hollywood 91606
TV commercial production and TV show development.
Jeff Newby, prod/director.

Newland–Raynor Productions, Inc   **(213) 655-2222**
8480 Beverly Blvd #133, Los Angeles 90048
F: features.

Nightingale Productions, Inc   **(619) 436-1051**
200 Nepture Ave, Encinitas 92024
F/V: shorts for education, inspiration. Main business: music production (Silver Nightingale Music). Joan Nemour, pres. (1975/2)

Wendell Niles Productions   **(818) 985-2252**
4555 Ledge Ave, North Hollywood 91602
V: TV series and specials including Youth Sings Out. (1965)

Noble Productions, Inc   **(213) 552-2984**
1615 South Crest Dr, Los Angeles 90035
F: features including Day of the Assassin, Winds of War. Also distribution. Ika Panajotovic, pres. (1966)

Harry Novak & Associates   213) 665-5257
4774 Melrose Ave, Los Angeles 90029
F: features. (1966)

November Productions   **(213) 652-1996**
204 S. Clark Drive, Beverly Hills 90211
F/V: TV specials. Penny Bigelow, pres. (1960)

The NRW Company   **(213) 856-1746**
5746 Sunset Blvd, Hollywood CA 90028
V: TV series Three's Company. Michael Ross, Benie West. George Sunga, exec in charge of production. (1977)

Nu Videa, Inc   **(213) 659-4037**
9165 Sunset Blvd #7, Los Angeles 90069
F/V: music videos, shorts. Also Music production, publishing, and licensing. Film/TV licensing and distribution. Gen Morita, pres., prod; Takeshi Kima, dir; Karen Deal, assoc prod. (1982/8)

O

October Productions, Inc (805) 962-2523
9 Ashley Ave, Santa Barbara 93103
F/V: commercials, shorts, features. Richard Hughes, pres.

Omega Pictures (213) 855-0516
8780 Shoreham Dr. #501, Los Angeles 90069
F: features including St. Killer's Day, The Wind. TV programing. Moderate budget features. Nico Mastorakis, pres; Richard George, dir (Europe); Robert Gilliam, exec vp. David Hirsch, vp production. (1974/43)

Omstar Productions (213) 464-6699
1714 N. Ivar Ave (North Wing), Los Angeles 90028
F/V: features including The Sky Is Falling, commercials, documentaries, B&I. Richard Skaggs, producer-creative director; Howard Sargent, producer.

On/SelectTV (213) 827-4400
4755 Alla Road, Marina del Rey 90291
Subscription TV serivce. Glen Meredith, programing.

Orion Pictures Corporation (213) 557-8700
1875 Century Park East, Los Angeles CA 90067
Feature development and financing with distribution through Warner Bros. Arthur Krim, chairman; Mike Medavoy, exec vp, Barbara Boyle, sen vp prod. Office also in NY. (1978)

Orion Television (213) 557-8700
1875 Century Park East, Los Angeles 90067
TV programing. Richard Rosenbloom, pres; Fred Whitehead vp development; Stan Neufeld, vp production; Gary Randall, vp TV development.

Eric Orner Productions (213) 467-8080
1965 N. Van Ness Ave, Los Angeles 90068
Theatrical and TV production. Eric Orner, prod/dir.

Glenn Otto Productions (213) 461-0222
937 N. Cole Ave (#2), Los Angeles 90038
F/V: B&I, commercials. (1966/2)

P

Pacific Electric Pictures   477-4504
1845 Pontius Ave, Los Angeles 90025
F: B&I, education, features. John Patrick Graham,
pres. (1979/7)

Pacific Films   (818) 848-5579
2530 N. Ontario, Burbank 91504
F: B&I, education. John Graham, pres. (1974/6)

Pacific Video Post Production Center   (213) 462-6266
809 N. Cahuenga Blvd, Los Angeles 90038
V: post production, all formats. Graphics; sweeten-
ing room, sound stage. Bob Seidenglanz, pres.
(1973/35)

Pacific Vitagraph   (213) 392-5165
P O Box 25165, West Los Angeles 90025
F: writing, production, consultation.

Paisano Productions, Inc   (213) 277-9482
9911 W. Pico PH E, Los Angeles 90035
F: Earle Stanley Gardner properties only.

The Pakula Company   (213) 208-3046
10889 Wilshire Blvd, #606, Los Angeles 90024
F: features including Starting Over. NY address:
445 Park Ave (8th Fl) NY (212) 208-3046. LA address
is producer-director Alan Pakula's accountant.

Palance-Levy Productions   (213) 467-7226
(Suite 32) 1438 N. Gower, Los Angeles 90028
F/V: features including The Sky's No Limit. Virginia
Palance, pres. (1977/4)

Pantomine Pictures, Inc   (818) 980-5555
12144 Riverside Dr, North Hollywood 91607
F: animation studio; commercials, TV series, features, shorts. Fred Crippen, dir-animator; Jack
Hadley, sales/producer. (1958/5)

Paramount Communications   (818) 240-9300
626 Justin Ave, North Hollywood 91201-2398
See: Aims Media

Paramount Pictures Corporation   (213) 468-5000
5555 Melrose Ave, Hollywood 90038
Frank Marcuso, chairman, CEO.

Paramount Pictures Motion Picture Group
Ned Tanen, pres. Distribution: Barry London, pres
domestic; Martin Kutner, exec vp international;
Allen Lewellen, exec vp general sales mgr; Jeffrey
Blake, vp domestic, Western division.

Paramount Pictures Production F: features
Dawn Steel, pres. David Kirkpatrick, exec vp; Steve
Bedell, vp music; Frank Bodo, vp finance; Lindsey
Doran, vp production; Charles Maguire vp exec pro-
duction mgr.

Paramount TV Group
Mel Harris, pres.

Paramount TV Production & Distribution
Ronald Nelson, pres.
TV series include Cheers, Family Ties, Webster.
Network: John Pike, exec vp network TV; Joyce
Brotman, vp comedy development; Thomas Daniels, vp
network daytime; Peter Greenberg, vp dramatic devel-
opment; Vickie Rosenberg, vp casting; Michael
Schoenbrun vp production.

Video: Roger Klingensmith, exec vp video distribution; Tim Clott, sen vp general mgr; Hollace Brown,
vp home video sales; Eric Doctorow, vp sales.

Paramount Domestic TV and Video Programming
W. Randolph Reiss, pres; John Goldhammer, exec vp
programing; Frank Kelly, vp programing

Paramount Studio Operations
Earl Lesz, pres.

Other divisions include: Famous Music Publishing,
Entertainment and Communication Group, International
Distribution Division.

Park Films Ltd   **(213) 652-6677**
8833 Sunset Blvd #307, Hollywood 90069
F: features including The Glory of Khan. Producers:
Sidney H. Levine, William Trowbridge, P. Moss.
(1985/12)

Park Lane Productions   **(21) 202-3368**
9336 W. Washington Blvd, Culver City 90232
Promotion of features. Also producer small features
and documentaries. Maria Dilon, owner/dir/prod;
Nancy Buys, admin. asst.

James D. Parriott Productions   **(818) 508-3171**
100 Universal City Plaza, Universal City 91608
Executive producer/writer/director.

Parvin-Rubalcava Productions   **(213) 828-1003**
1444 Berkeley Apt. E, Santa Monica 90404
F: features. Ted Parvin, pres. (1979)

Pasetta Productions   **(213) 655-8500**
8322 Beverly Blvd. #205, Los Angeles 90048
V: music/variety specials, award shows, and events.
(1970)

Paulist Productions   **(213) 454-0688**
P O Box 1057, Pacific Palisades 90272
F/V: TV series (Insight); programing of educational-
religious nature including The Fourth Wise Man. Fr.
Elwood Kieser, exec prod; producers: Mike Rhodes and
Lewis Abel. (1960/20)

Pavel Productions, Inc   **(818) 762-5848**
11927 Magnolia Blvd #18, North Hollywood 91607
Motion picture and stage productions. Films range
from documentaries to features. Foreign contacts,
mostly German, Austrian, and East European film
companies. Pavel Cerny, prod/dir; Helena
Weltman/Cerny, assoc prod, literary manager (1976).

Pavillion Communications   **(213) 466-9351**
6245 Afton Place, Hollywood 90028
Rental: studio, equipment. Shinya Egawa, pres; Yucca
Comelli, administration.

Pegboard Productions   **(818) 353-4991**
13104 Helendale Ave., Tujunga 91042
F: animation; features, commercials, shorts. Becky
Bristow, animator/dir; Elrene Cowan, producer.
(1978/3)

People to People Films   **(213) 854-4364**
12077 Wilshire Blvd. #530, Los Angeles 90025
F/V: features, live and tape TV shows, music videos,
documentaries.   Full feature production house with
union & nonunion crews. Debbie Martone, prod, production mgr; Eric Jones, writer, prod, dir. (1983)

Petersen Communications   **(213) 874-3400**
7656 Sunset Blvd, Hollywood 90046
F: B&I, commercials, documentaries. (1982)

The Phoenix Company   **(818) 508-4913**
100 Universal City Plaza, 69-F, Universal City 91608
F: features including Rustles Rhapsody. David Giler,
Walter Hill. (1976)

Pierre Enterprises, Inc   **(213) 937-6764**
1164 S. La Brea Ave, Los Angeles 90019
F: commercials. Pierre O. Ninomiya, pres. (1980/4)

Ping Pong Productions   **(213) 653-7028**
7471 Melrose Ave #11, Los Angeles 90046
F: commercials, features, documentaries, B&I. M.J.
Carazza, pres; T.J. Castronova, vp; Val Safarik, exec
prod. (1977)

Playboy Productions   **(213) 659-4080**
8560 Sunset Blvd, Los Angeles 90069
F/V: features, TV series, specials. Michael
Brandman, pres; Edward Rissien, development. Playboy
Cable at same address.

Playhouse Pictures   **(213) 851-2112**
1401 N. La Brea Ave, Hollywood 90028
F: features, commercials, animation. Ted Woolery,
producer. (1952/12)

The Polished Apple   **(213) 459-2630**
3742 Seahorn Dr, Malibu 90265
F/FS: education. R.J. Wilhite, pres. (1973/7)

Sydney Pollack   (818) 954-1711
Mirage Enterprises, 4000 Warner Blvd, Burbank 91522
F: features including Absence of Malice, Tootsie.
Sydney Pollack, producer-director.

PolyGram Pictures   (213) 202-4400
3940 Overland Ave, Culver City 90230
F: features including A Chorus Line.

Potpourri Productions   (213) 275-4683
8558 W. 3rd St, Los Angeles 90048
V: concept development: musical productions. Choreo-
graphy-live stage shows; nite club revues.   Knych
Keller; Perimeg Judith. (1979/2)

Praxis Film Works   (818) 508-0402
6918 Tujunga Ave, North Hollywood 91605
Special visual effects: features (Star Wars), commercials, TV. Robert Blalack, pres; Nancy Rushlow,
exec prod; Charles Alvare, marketing. (1980/15)

Premiere International   (213) 652-9354
8721 Sunset Blvd, Los Angeles 90069
Distributor: features. See: The Carlin Company.

Premore, Inc   (213) 506-7714
5130 Klump Ave, North Hollywood 91601
V: TV. Also post-production facility.

Edward R. Pressman Productions, Inc   (818) 954-3315
4000 Warner Blvd (Producers 5), Burbank 91522
F: features including Conan the Barbarian.

Prestige Pictures Releasing Corp.   (213) 466-5668
1765 N. Highland Ave, Hollywood 90028
F: features; production and distribution.

Prism Productions   (818) 703-1227
P O Box 83, Canoga Park 91305
F/V: TV series, documentaires, shorts. Specialty is
making science and technology understood. Don
Herbert (Mr. Wizard), producer; Norma Herbert, mar-
keting. (1952/3)

Producers Associates   **(213) 851-4123**
7243 Santa Monica Blvd, Hollywood 90046
F/V: commercials, promotional films; radio spots.
Original music. Complete video post production facility. Jack Spear, dir; Larry Frank, assoc producer; Robin Alison, production coordinator.

Producers Sales Organization   **(213) 552-9977**
10100 Santa Monica Blvd. #1580, Los Angeles 90067
Woldwide promotion, distribution, and sales repre-
sentation of feature films in all media. Mark Damon,
chairman.   TLX:698652

Production 8 Corporation   **(213) 469-5165**
1800 N. Highland Ave. #410, Hollywood 90028
V: Japanese production company shooting commercials
for the LA market and programing for Japan. (1976)

Project Films   **(213) 274-8708**
9744 Wilshire Blvd #207, Beverly Hills 90212
F/V: commercials, B&I. Special visual effects; por-
table special effects camera sleds. Ernie Andrews,
pres; Palmer Packard, general man. (1967)

The Puppet Works   **(213) 463-1640**
2677 N. Beachwood Dr, Hollywood 90068
F/V: commercials, B&I, education. Puppets, puppet-
eers, puppet effects. Greg Williams, pres. (1978/10)

John Purdy, Inc   **(213) 874-9802**
2307 Castilian Dr, Los Angeles 90068
Commercials, B&I, education. John Purdy, dir-producer; Gail Wilson, producer; Jack Black, production
mgr.

Pyramid Film & Video   **(213) 828-7577**
2801 Colorado Ave, Santa Monica 90404
F/V: shorts, every categroy. Distributor of over 500
titles. Domestic and worldwide distribution: 37
international sub-distributors. David Adams, pres;
Lynn Adams vp. (1959/39)

Q

Q-ED Productions, Inc   **(818) 991-3290**
P O Box 4029, Westlake Village 91359
F/V/FS: education. James L. Friedrich, pres.
(1947/13)

Q-M Productions   **(213) 208-2000**
10960 Wilshire Blvd, Los Angeles 90024
F/V: TV series, features, specials. A division of
Taft Broadcasting.

Quartet Films   **(818) 509-0100**
12345 Ventura Blvd. #M, Studio City 91604
F: commercials; animation and live action. Michael
Lah, pres. (1953/9)

R

Rainbow TV Works   **(213) 469-1611**
1420 N. Beachwood Dr, Los Angeles 90028
F/V: TV features and specials. Topper Carew, exec
producer. (1977/18)

Raintree Productions, Ltd   **(213) 652-8330**
666 N. Robertson Blvd, Los Angeles 90069
F/V: TV commercials. Robert Wollin, pres, prod; Jack
Howard, vp, general man; Kari Rantala, production.
(1975/6)

Raleigh Studio   **(213) 466-3111**
650 N. Bronson Ave, Los Angeles 90004
Rental: sound stages, lighting, post production,
screening. Norman Barnett vp general mgr. (1979)

Ramsey Enterprises, Inc   **(213) 393-9797**
719 Georgina, Santa Monica 90402
F/V: features, TV series, commercials. (1970)

Random Productions   (818) 760-7333
5437 Laurel Canyon Blvd, North Hollywood 91607
V: TV variety, series. Stuart Schoenburg, pres.
(1970)

Martin Ransohoff Productions   (818) 954-3491
300 Colgems Square, Burbank 91505
F: features including Class.

Rastar   (818) 954-2741
Columbia Plaza West, Burbank 91505
F: features and TV series including Blue Thunder.
Divisions: Rastar Films, Rastar TV. (1973/65)

R C T Productions   (213) 737-2199
3503 Venice Blvd, Los Angeles 90019
F/V: features, documentaries, and commercials. Pro-
duction crews available. Romeo L. Taylor, pres; C.M.
Wiliams, general man; Lee Blake, development; Romeo
Valtino Taylor, general mgr. (1975/12)

RDR Productions   (213) 205-0666
260 S. Beverly Dr, Beverly Hills 90212
F: independent feature production company (including
Death of an Angel), the Navigator). Dimitri Villard,
pres; Robby Wald, exec vp.

Rearguard Productions, Inc   (213) 937-1570
6030 Wilshire Blvd. #300, Los Angeles
F: features and distribution. Max Rosenberg, pres;
Julie Moldo, vp; W.J. Sobaka, development.

Robert Redford See: Wildwood Enterp   (818) 994-3788

The Reibold Company   (213) 462-3209
3410 N. Knoll Dr, Los Angeles 90068
F/V; commercials, B&I. Celebrity packaging. Dick
Reibold, pres. (1969)

Reid Miles, Inc   (213) 462-6106
1136 N. Las Palmas, Hollywood 90038
F: commercials. Still photography. (1973)

Retina Productions   (818) 366-2780
P O Box 33161, Granada Hills 91344
F: shorts; low budget features for cable. Set construction. Larry Paul Van Loon, pres; Robert Havens,
vp. (1971)

Review Educational Films (213) 947-7000
13743 Victory Blvd, Van Nuys 91401
F: education. A division of Don Stern Productions.
(1971/3)

Burt Reynolds See: Deliverance Prod. (818) 954-2496

Joe Reynolds Film Maker (213) 469-4375
1136 N. Tamarind Ave, Hollywood 90038
F/V: B&I. (1970)

RFG Associates, Inc (213) 466-2648
1530 N Gower St, #204, Hollywood 90028
F/V: consultation and production for B&I, TV, theatre. Teleconferencing. Duke Goldstone, pres.

Rhodes Productions (213) 379-3686
124 Eleventh St, Manhattan Beach 90266
V: TV series. Also distributor. Jack Rhodes, pres;
William G. Rhodes, vp-special projects; Chris
Remington, sales.

Riviera Productions (818) 889-5778
31628 Saddletree Dr, Westlake Village 91361
F: features, commercials, TV series. F.W. Zens, exec
producer; Leif Rise, assoc producer.

Hal Roach Studios, Inc (213) 850-0525
1600 N. Fairfax, Hollywood 90046
F/V: features and TV. Earl Glick, chairman; Victor
White, production; Norman Glenn & Jules Sack, sales.
(1982)

Ronox Productions (213) 851-1880
2217 Chelan Dr, Los Angeles 90068
F/V: documentaries for TV. (1969)

Ted Roter, Film & Stage Productions (213) 473-3559
12211 Malone St, Los Angeles 90066
Film/tape productions. Ted Roter, pres. (1975/4)

Roundtable Films, Inc   **(213) 657-1402**
113 N. San Vicente Blvd, Beverly Hills 90211
F/V/M: B&I, government. Distribution; many titles in foreign languages. Leon Gold, pres, Kenneth Newelt, operations; Pat Davies, new product development. (1958)

Jack Rourke Productions   **(213) 843-4889**
P O Box 1705, Burbank 91507
F/V: commercials, B&I. (195/10)

Roven Productions   **(213) 276-6180**
PO Box 5192, Beverly Hills 90210
F: development & production of motion pictures. Charles Roven, pres/prod; Lois Gore, asst.

Royalty Reels   **(213) 467-5386**
650 N. Bronson Ave, Los Angeles 90004
F/V: features, especially Spanish language, B&I. (1978/4)

Ruby-Spears Enterprises, Inc   **(213) 874-5100**
3255 Cahuenga Blvd West, Los Angeles 90068
F: animated TV series including Mister T, specials. Joseph Ruby, chairman, exec producer; Kenneth Spears, pres; exec producer; Harriet Beck, vp-business affairs; Richard Leary, communications

Ruddy-Morgan Productions   **(213) 271-7698**
120 El Camino #204, Beverly Hills 90212
F: features including Megaforce. Albert Ruddy, Andre Morgan.

Aaron Russo Productions, Inc   **(213) 558-6738**
10202 W. Washington Blvd, Culver City 90230
F: features including Trading Places, Teachers. (1979)

Michael Ryan Productions, Inc   **(818) 704-7316**
P O Box 6576, Woodland Hills 91365
F: features. (1983/3)

S

S & A Productions (Sullivan & Assoc) (213) 384-3331
201 N. Occidental Blvd, Los Angeles 90026
F/V: TV cable; S & A Studios rents sound stages.
Larry Sullivan, pres; Roger Nichols, vp. (1973/40)

Sagen Arts, Inc (213) 851-1661
7631 Lexington Ave, Los Angeles 90046
V: TV series, primarily children and family entertainment with emphasis on comedy. Stu Rosen, pres.
(1970/3)

Salenger Films (213) 450-1300
1635 12th St, Santa Monica 90404
F/V: Produce, acquire, and distribute management and
sales training. Fred Salenger, pres; Susan Salenger
exec vp.

Leo Salkin Films, Inc (213) 463-4513
6305 Yucca (#500), Los Angeles 90028
F: animation; features, commercials, TV specials
including Two-Thousand-Year-Old Man. (1971)

Salzburg Enterprises (213) 558-4688
10070 Culver Blvd, Culver City 90230
Cable and TV programing. Milton Salzburg, pres.

Ron Samuels Productions (818) 954-6431
3903 W. Olive (#322), Burbank 91522
F: features including Callie & Son.

Sanrio Communications, Inc (213) 470-8500
10474 Santa Monica Blvd, #301, Los Angeles 90025
Distribution of animated features. Part of Sanrio
Company, Ltd, Tokyo. Etsuo Iida, managing dir;
Sachiko Louie, sales. (1975/14)

Jim Sant'Andrea Inc (213) 979-9100
855 W. Victoria St(LA Industrl Cntr), Compton 90220
F/V/S/M & special effects: B&I, education, entertainment. NY office. Ron Neter, producer; Guy Hence,
general man. (1971/10)

Pierre Sauvage Productions   (213) 650-8986
8760 Wonderland Ave, Los Angeles 90046
F/V: special and series for network and cable TV.
(1979)

Saxton Films   (213) 654-4364
1422 N. Sweetzer, Los Angeles 90069
F: features. Distribution also. Robert Saxton, pres;
David Edward, vp. (1978/7)

Schaefer/Karpf Productions   (818) 506-6655
12711 Ventura Blvd #307, Studio City 91607
Independent TV production company. George Schaefer,
dir; Merrill H. Karpf, exec prod.

Lawrence Schiller Productions   (818) 906-0926
4827 N. Sepulveda Blvd, Sherman Oaks 91403
F: features and TV programing, including The Execu-
tioner's Song. (1979)

George Schlatter Productions   (213) 655-1400
8321 Beverly Blvd, Los Angeles 90048
Film/tape producer.

Gerald Schnitzer Productions   (213) 657-7380
1155 N. La Cienega Blvd, Los Angeles 90069
TV and motion picture production; creative consultants. Writing, desgining TV commercials, documentaries, etc. Gerald Schnitzer, exec prod.

Robert Schnitzer Productions, Inc.   (213) 850-1122
7135 Hollywood Blvd, #709, Los Angeles 90046
F/V: features (including Rebel) and TV programing.
Robert Schnitzer, pres (1968/6)

Schulman Video Center   (213) 465-8110
861 Seward St, Hollywood 90038
V: Remote, studio, and editing facilities for broadcast and non-broadcast productions.

Randal Schultz Video   (213) 399-1101   (714) 857-1310
223 Strand St #K, Santa Monica 90405
V: 5% commercials, 40% informationals, 50% industrials, 5% specials. Randal Schultz, exec prod, dir;
Liliane Pelzman, prod, assoc dir. (1979/6)

Bernard Schwart Productions　　　　**(818) 508-3283**
Bldg 507 3G, Universal Studios, Universal City 91608
Feature film and TV production. Carlton Cuse, prod.

Science Concepts　　　　**(213) 397-8245**
3455 Meier St, Los Angeles 90066
F/V/M: producer of science and technical material;
time-lapse, electronic & computer technology. Stock
footage and slides. Steve Craig.

Security Pictures, Inc　　　　**(619) 454-2363**
8315 Camino del Oro, La Jolla 90327
F: features. Mr. Yordan, pres.

Select Video, Inc.　　　　**(213) 993-5322**
P O Box 1055, Northridge CA 91324
Distributors of videotape pre-recorded cassettes:
including children's, general, and adult.

S-G Productions, Inc　　　　**(213) 849-2471**
3400 W. Alamdea Ave, #100, Burbank 91505
V: TV specials including Dean Martin Special. Greg
Garrison, exec producer; Lee Hale, producer. (1965)

Jack Shafton Productions　　　　**(818) 985-5025**
5500 Clean Ave, North Hollywood 91601
Fabricators of props and costumes. Ted Burleson.

Bea Shaw Productions　　　　**(818) 761-9857**
10527 Sarah St, North Hollywood 91602
Commercials. (1963)

Edward Shaw Productions　　　　**(818) 705-8760**
P O Box 709, Woodland Hills 91365
F/V: features, commercials, B&I, education. Brandy
Allor, program development. (1970/10)

David Sheldon　　　　**(213) 652-6263**
1437 Rising Glen Rd, Los Angeles 90069
F: producer-director of features including Lovely
But Deadly. (1974)

Tom Shelley Enterprises　　　　**(213) 466-4650**
6253 Hollywood Blvd. #603, Hollywood 90028
F: PSA, commercials, shorts. Main business is adver-
tising/public relations. Announcing and VO. (1973/1)

The Richard Shepherd Company (213) 820-7751
Lion's Gate, 1861 S. Bundy Dr, Los Angeles 90025
F: features including Volunteers.

Sherwood Productions (213) 205-7500
9454 Wilshire Blvd. #309, Beverly Hills 90212
F: features including Mr. Mom. Bruce McNall (1981)

Shoemaker Productions (714) 261-2311
18001 Skypark Circle #R, Irvine 92714
F/V: commercials, sports & fashion specials, features. Specialize in camera mounts, helicopter, all action sports production (Action Now - TV series). Don Shoemaker, pres; Dave DAsh, prod; Kevin Hartwell, marketing. (1968/6)

Showtime/The Movie Channel (213) 208-2340
10900 Wilshire Blvd, Los Angeles 90024
Pay TV serivce. Brad Johnson, vp-current programing; Peter Chernin, exec vp, programing; Development: Allen Sabinson Sr, vp, program dev; Stuart Smiley, special events; Natalie Seaver, drama; Richard Albarino, comedy; Emmy Torres.

The Sidaris Company (213) 275-2682
1891 Carla Ridge, Beverly Hills 90210
F/V: features including Seven. (1967)

Silent Network (213) 654-6972
P.O. Box 1902, Beverly Hills 90213
Information & entertainment programing in sign language, voice, and open caption for deaf and hearing audiences. Sheldon Altfeld, pres/exec prod; Carol Mau, vp, sales; Lawrence Pike vp, satellite operations.

Silvereagle Productions (818) 703-6234
22277 1/2 Erwin St., Woodland Hills 91367
F: TV movies, commercials, music videos, and B&I. Post production. Bret Hampton, exec prod, dir; Greg Tatum, prod, dir. (1983)

Silver/Regan Productions (213) 559-0346
9336 W. Washington Blvd, Culver City 90230
Produce and supervise production on independent features, MOWs, cable series, commercials, and music videos. Alain Silver, prod; Patrick Regan, producer.

Al Simon Productions   **(213) 464-9216**
5858 Hollywood Blvd. #403, Hollywood 90028
F: TV programing.

Melvin Simon Productions, Inc   **(213) 273-5450**
260 S. Beverly Dr, Beverly Hills 90212
F: features. Melvin Simon, pres; Milton Goldstein,
CEO; John F. Rubinich vp, worldwide sales; Dayle
Michelle vp creative affairs. (1982)

Nicholas Simone Productions   **(213) 661-7777**
444 S. Victory Blvd, Burbank 91502
A music and sound design facility offering synthesis
of film and commercial scoring, special effects,
computerized sound composition. Featuring Digital
Production Music Library.

Jerry Sims Productions   **(818) 766-4363**
3765 Cahuenga Blvd. West, Studio City 91604
F/V: commercials. Jerry Sims, dir; Gordon Gadette,
exec prod; Lala Aquilar, sales/Int'l prod. (1973)

Siroco Enterprises   **(213) 276-1014**
9200 Sunset Blvd, Los Angeles 90069
F/V: TV series including The Norm Crosby Comedy
Shop. Joe Siegman & Perry Rosemond, producers.
(1977)

Size Inc   **(213) 223-2312**
600 Moulton Ave #405, Los Angeles 90031
F: Commercials for Japan. Alvin Mori, exec prod; Jay
Tsukamoto, prod; Hideo Oida, prod.

Skip Ishii Productions, Inc (SIP)   **(213) 617-3336**
305 Boyd St, Los Angeles 90013
F: commercials. Skip Ishii, pres. (1976/8)
FAX (213) 617-0741

Skipsey & Associates   **(213) 465-3232**
650 N. Bronson Ave, Los Angeles 90004
Still photography. No F/V.

Skylight Productions   **(213) 464-4500**
6815 Willoughby Ave. #201, Los Angeles 90038
Off-line video and film editing. Specialty: projects
shot on film and finished in tape. Barbara Ottinger.
(1978/3)

Skyline Productions   (213) 856-0033
6309 Eleanor St, Hollywood 90038
F/V: sound service. Sound equipment: sales & rental,
design and manufacture. Dean Gilmore, pres; Blake
Wilcox, vp; Phil Silver, general mgr; Tim Holly
service mgr; Fred Ginsburg, marketing. (1966/4)

S-L Film Productions   (213) 254-8528
P O Box 41108, Los Angeles 90041
F/V: education, documentary. Sound recording. Gerald
Schiller, pres. (1966.3)

Smith-Hemion Productions   (213) 871-1200
1438 N. Gower, Los Angeles 90028
F/V: TV variety shows. Gary Smith & Dwight Hemion;
Jerry Katz, manager. (1962)

Snowflake Films Inc   (213) 461-4798
1607 N. El Centro, Los Angeles 90028
Producers, directors; post production. Joe
Robertson, pres.

Solar Survival   (213) 392-9551
1920 Main St, Santa Monica 90405
F: features including Fade to Black, Surf II. Producers: George Braunstein, Ron Hamady.

Soldenski Productions   (818) 957-2292
4415 Ocean View,Montrose 91020
F/V: religious shorts.

The SoloFilm Company   (213) 858-8689
9507 S. Monica Blvd, Beverly Hills 90210
Motion picture production.

Andrew Solt Productions   (213) 276-9522
9113 Sunset Blvd, Los Angeles 90069
F: features, variety specials including Prime Time.
(1977/5)

Richard J. Soltys Productions   (818) 843-0373
1615 W. Burbank Blvd, Burbank 91506
F/V: B&I; some internally produced educational films
distributed through Informational Materials Inc.
Richard J. Soltys, owner. (1959/4)

Leonard South Productions (818) 760-8383
4500 Forman Ave, Toluca Lake 91602
F/V/M: B&I. (1969)

Southerby Productions (213) 498-6088
5000 East Anaheim St, Long Beach 90804
Distribution educational films/video. John Whalley,
vp sales; Norm Southerby, pres.

Rick Spalla Video Productions (RSVP) (213) 469-7307
1622 N Gower St, Los Angeles 90028
F/V: commercials, B&I, education, music video; satellite syndication; live programing. Offline 16mm &
videotape editing. Rick Spalla, pres; Jeff Spalla,
production supervisor. (1952/6)

Aaron Spelling Productions (213) 850-3911
1041 N. Formosa, Hollywood 90046
F: TV series (exec prod) Love Boat, Dynasty, Matt
Houston, MacGruder & Loud. Aaron Spelling, pres,
exec producer; Douglas S. Cramer, vp, exec producer.

Spiegel-Bergman Productions, Inc (213) 552-0577
2029 Century Park East (#1850), Los Angeles 90067
F: features.

The Ed Spiegel Company (213) 874-3362
8489 W. Third St, Los Angeles 90048
F/V: features and documentaries.

Steve Spielberg (818) 508-4600
Universal Stuido Bldg 447, Universal City 91608
F: features including E.T. and TV series (Amazing
Stories).

Jack Spear Productions (213) 851-4123
7243 Santa Monica Blvd, Los Angeles 90046
F/V: Full service TV and radio production company
specializing in materials for industry and education. Facilities: audio studio, 16 and 35mm editing
rooms, insert stage, 3/4" offline and 1" on-line
video editing bays. Jack Spear, pres./dir; Larry
Frank, prod., production manager; Melissa Jenkins,
production asst; Julie Brayton, editor.

Milton Sperling Productions   (818) 981-4313
13701 Riverside Dr. #400, Sherman Oaks 91423
F: features for theatre and TV. Milton Sperling,
pres.

Spungbuggy Works, Inc   (213) 657-8070
8506 Sunset Blvd, Los Angeles 90069
F/V: commercials: live action, animation, the two
combined. Herb Stott, pres; Larry Catusi, sales;
David Persoff, producer; Kris Weber, animat.-produ-
cer. (1963)

SRS Communications   (818) 996-5337
4224 Ellenita Ave, Tarzana 91356
F/V: documentaries, features, shorts. Denis Sanders,
pres; Arthur Swerdloff, vp. (1974/7)

Stage Fright Productions   (818) 768-3333
8817 Amboy Ave, Sun Valley 91352
F/V: complete production for B&I market. David L.
Phyfer, prod/dir; John Kelly, dir/writer.

The Stanfield House   (213) 820-4568
12381 Wilshire Blvd. #203, Los Angeles 90025
F/V/FS: education. Distribution also; some captioned. Diane Stanfield. (1972/3)

Kris Stevens Enterprises   (818) 981-8255
14241 Ventura Blvd. #204, Sherman Oaks 91423
F/V: commercials for TV and radio. Facilities: recording studios, sound effects, music library, 3/4
video capabilities. Kris Erik Stevens, pres; Doree
Glaser, prod; Technical engineers: Terry Harris,
Christopher Hartt; Sue Steinberg, operations mgr.

Star Cinema Production Group, Inc   (213) 463-2000
6253 Hollywood Blvd, #830, Hollywood 90028
F: features including Malibu High. Seminars & on
location apprenticeship programs. Lawrence Foldes,
pres; Victoria Paige Meyerink, vp. (1977/4)

The Peter Starr Production Company   (818) 888-2500
23320 Oxnard St. Woodland Hills 91367
F/V: action sports documentaries and features, uti-
lizing point of view photography. Peter Starr, pres.
(1973/15)

Steckler Productions   **(213) 275-8647**
9530 Heather Road, Beverly Hills 90210
F: TV series and features; within budgetary demands.
(1966)

Don Stern Productions   **(818) 994-7000**
13743 Victory Blvd, Van Nuys 91401
F/V: services other production companies with facilities and personnel: pre production, production,
post production in all film/tape formats. Don Stern,
producer-dir. (1960/14)

The Robert Stigwood Org. (RSO Films) **(213) 468-5802**
5555 Melrose Ave, Hollywood 90038
F: features. (1974)

Bob Stivers Associates   **(213) 467-4000**
710 N. Seward, Los Angeles 90038
V: TV specials including Circus of the Stars. Bob
Stivers, producer; Julian Bercovici, production.
(1976/20)

Andre Stojka Productions   **(213) 934-5906**
1246 S. La Cienega Blvd, Los Angeles 90035
F/S/V: B&I, cable. Music tracking for other companies. (1976)

Andrew L. Stone, Inc   **(213) 279-2427**
10478 Wyton Dr, Los Angeles 90024
F: features. (1955)

Storer Cable Communications   **(818) 889-0282**
30901 Agoura Rd, Westlake Village 91361
Cable franchise with local origination and access
channels. Studio and mobile production van; 3/4 "
edit bay. Rental of facilities. Ray Hinton Jr,
production coordinator.

The Story Company   **(415) 626-0565**
301 8th St #210, San Francisco 94103
F/V: commercials, B&I; animation, live action,
titles. (1969/10)

Herbert L. Strock Productions   **(213) 421-1298**
6500 Barton Ave, Hollywood 90038
F/V: commercials, features, shorts. Editing. Sound
transfer. Neg cutting; sound effects, music editing.
Herbert Strock, producer.

Studio Animatics (213) 933-0646
801 N. La Brea Ave, #104, Los Angeles 90038
Specialty: animatics and photomatics for test commercials and client presentations. Producer of animated commercials and shorts. Jim Keeshen, prod/dir.

The Milton B. Suchin Company (213) 550-1133
201 N. Robertson Blvd #A, Beverly Hills 90211
Personal management and production. Supervising producer of The Most Watchable Man Contest. Exec. assts: Susan Powers, Laura Aryan.

Burt Sugarman, Inc (213) 273-0900
Beverly Wilshire Hotel, Beverly Hills 90212
F/V: TV series and features.

Sun Productions (213) 820-8236
818 Gretna Green Way (#109), Los Angeles 90049
F/V:features, commercials, B&I, education. Paul Nobert, producer. (1970/4)

Sunbreak Productions, Inc (213) 659-2324
256 S. La Cienega Blvd, Beverly Hills 90211
F/V: features, TV programing, B&I, commercials. William Mauger, exec prod; Dennis Aubrey, dir, prod. (1978)

Sunrise Canyon Video (818) 845-7473
PO Box 10968, Burbank 91510
V: 3/4 & 1" Betacam services and production crews; stage with grid. Specialize in remote location photography. William Hughes, owner (1975/4)

Sunwest Productions, Inc (213) 461-2957
1021 N. Mc Cadden Place, Hollywood 90038
F/V: commercials, features, shorts. Live action and animation. International ties in Paris, Tokyo, Mexico City. Richard Jackson, pres; Lynne Jackson, producer; Richard Haboush, exec producer; Hal Greenfader & Kit Hudson, directors. (1974/16)
TWX:910-321-2834

Supercolossal Pictures Corporation (213) 876-6770
3413 Cahuengal Blvd West, Los Angeles 90068
V/F: Commercials, B&I, education. Sound stage, recording studios, mobile videotape truck. Warren Deasy, pres. (1970)

Super-Vision   (213) 464-2536
590 N. Rossmore Ave, Los Angeles 90004
F/V: movies. Manufacture of Super-Vision optical
system. Will develop features with 50% financing.
Barnard Sackett, pres; Gloria Geale, production man;
Peter Morrocu, vp. (1976/25)

Suski/Fallick Productions, Inc   (213) 462-2171
6671 Sunset Blvd. Bldg. 1574, Hollywood 90028
F/V: feature film promotion in all media; foreign &
domestic. George Suski; Mort Fallick. (1974/6)

Sutherland Learning Associates, Inc   (818) 701-1344
8700 Reseda Blvd. #108, Northridge 91324
F: shorts in fields of medicine and education. Distribution. Publisher medical material. (1943/20)

Swanson Productions, Inc   (213) 851-8930
2811 Cahuenga Blvd West, Hollywood 90068
F/V: commercials. Glen Swanson, dir; Joanne
Dimattia, producer.

Sweetwater Productions, Inc   (818) 954-1691
4000 Warner Blvd, Burbank 91505
F: feature. Michael Cimino.

T

D. L. Taffner, Ltd   (213) 937-1144
5455 Wilshire Blvd #1908, Los Angeles 90036
F/V: producer TV series Too Close for Comfort. Distributes Three's Company. Don Taffner, pres. NY
office: (212) 245-4680. (1970/45)

The Taft Entertainment Company   (213) 208-2000
10960 Wilshire Blvd, 10th Flr, Los Angeles 90024
Sy Fischer, pres; Subsidiaries: Taft Entertainment
Television (all TV programing. W. Russell Barry,
pres), Hanna Barbera, Ruby-Spears, Titus Productions
(NY), Sunn Classic (Salt Lake).

Tamarand Films, Inc   **(213) 461-5100**
1124 N. Citrus Ave, Los Angeles 90038
F/V: commercials, B&I, documentaries. Dan Lindquist,
pres-dir; Finn Myggen, exec prod. (1974)

Tandem Productions, Inc
Corp: 1901 Ave of the Stars, LA 90067 (213) 553-3600
Studio: 1438 N. Gower, Hollywood 90028   460-7200
Division of Embassy Communications.
F: TV series Different Strokes.

Tauro Productions   **(213) 258-2379**
5019 York Blvd, Los Angeles 90042
F/V: Spanish language commercials. Translation,
dubbing. Alex Tauro, Al Vincent. (1957/3)

Larry Taylor Productions   **(818) 798-6546**
2919 Sterling Place, Altadena 91001
F: features, all genres, budgets $1-3 million. Also
produce TV series, pilots. Opening European style TV
commercial production house. Larry Taylor, pres.,
prod/dir/OOO; Robert H. Robinson, vp creative affairs, Irene Solf, client liaison; Jeffrey L.
Blazeff, public relations.

The Burbank Studios (TBS)   **(818) 954-6000**
4000 Warner Blvd, Burbank 91522
Home of Warner Bros. and Columbia Pictures. First
total production center with sate-of-the-art film,
videotape, and music recording facilities staffed by
technically skilled personnel. All production sup-
port and post production facilities. 38 sound
stages; production vans; outdoor sets; scoring
stages, dubbing stages. Gary Paster, pres; Ronald
Stein vp production services; Vince Hedge, studio
services. (1972)

TCA Films   **(213) 540-2165**
21417 Evalyn Ave, Torrance 90503
F/V: commercials, B&I, education. (1972)

Teleklew Productions, Inc   **(213) 451-5727**
1299 Ocean Ave. #800, Santa Monica 90401
V: TV programing. (1955)

Telepictures Corporation   **(213) 659-7794**
415 N. Crescent Dr. #300, Beverly Hills 90211
F/V: TV programing (including Ellis Island, Rituals). Distributor syndicated TV programing to stations, airlines, non-broadcast, cable TV, pay TV. Frank Konigsberg, pres; Larry Sanitsky, vp creative affairs; Jack Clements, vp production. (1978/65)

Ten-Four Productions, Inc   **(213) 655-9470**
8271 Melrose Ave, Los Angeles 90046
F: TV features (including He's Not Your Son) and series, including Falcon Crest (1976/14). Sam Strangis, pres; Greg Strangis, vp.

Third Eye Production Company   **(213) 854-4939**
100 S. Doheny (#222), Los Angeles 90048
F: features; TV for European broadcast. Finance and distribution. Frederic Golchan, pres. (1978)

Third Wave Productions   **(213) 851-1636**
7130 Hollywood Blvd, #22, Los Angeles 90046
V/F: commercials, B&I, specials for cable including Course in Miracles. Specialty: musical promotionals/dance choreography spots. William J. Murray, pres; Terry Kearney, vp, June Dante, producer, Chris Landry, production mgr. (1982/4)

Danny Thomas Productions   **(818) 985-2940**
11350 Ventura Blvd., Studio City 91604
F: TV and features. Exec prods: Danny Thomas, Ronald Jacobs.

Thorn EMI Screen Entertainment Inc   **(213) 278-4770**
9229 Sunset Blvd, 9th Flr, Los Angeles 90069
Corporate title: Thorn EMI (Great Britain); Verity Lambert, film production; Robert Webster, product acquisiton. Subsidiaries: Thorn EMI TV Programs, EMI Films.
F/V: programs for TV. Robert Gimbel, exec producer; Tony Converse, exec producer; Karen Jones, story editor.

Threshold Films   **(213) 874-8413**
2025 N Highland Ave, Los Angeles 90068
16mm sales & rental: features, shorts. Worldwide distribution for TV and cable.

Thursday's Child Productions   (213) 874-4427
7245 Franklin Ave #17, Los Angeles 90046-3027
F/TV: production services including management, accounting. Also superloopers, a voice-over, looping and dubbing group. Norman Marcus, owner/prod; Devera Marcus, dubbing.

Tisch/Avnet Productions, Inc   (213) 278-7680
515 N. Robertson Blvd, Los Angeles 90048
F: features including Coast to Coast and TV programing. Steve Tisch; John Avnet.

C. Tobalina Productions, Inc   (213) 749-2067
1044 S. Hill St, Los Angeles 90015
F/V: adult features. Distribution by assoc. company: HIFCOA. E. Tobalina, pres. (1963/48)

Tobenkin Productions   (213) 659-9863
927 N. La Cienega, W. Hollywood 90069
Commercials. Steven Tobenkin, exec prod; directors: Kent Wakeford, Olivier Karsenty, Alan Metter.

The Toho Company   (213) 277-1081
2049 Century Pk East #490, Los Angeles 90067
F: production, distribution, import and export. Satoru Terada, mgr.

Tomarken Productions   (213) 203-2871
PO Box 900, Beverly Hills 90213
F: TV and feature production. Peter Tomarken, principal.

Tomorrow Entertainment   (718) 361-0077
34-31 35th St, Astoria NY 11106
F/V: TV production for network, cable, pay TV. F: features. John Backe, chairman; Myron Hyman, pres. Peggy Lamont, vp development.

Trancas International Films, Inc   (213) 657-7670
9229 Sunset Blvd. #415, Los Angeles 90069
F: low budget features. (1964)

Trans-American Video, Inc   (213) 466-2141
1541 N. Vine St, Hollywood 90028
V: full service facility: stage, mobile units. Division of Merv Griffin Productions. Jeff Ross, sales. (1978/100)

Trans-Atlantic Enterprises   (213) 454-6515
101 Ocean Ave, Santa Monica 90402
F: miniseries, documentaries, specials. Robert Kline, pres; Leonard Freidlander, vp production; Lyndie White, production coordinator.

Trans World International, Inc   (213) 477-8561
11050 Santa Monica Blvd, Los Angeles 90025
F/V: sports; staged events and films about sports. Arthur Rosenblum, sen vp. (1966/40)

Translor Films, Inc   (213) 274-8488
9200 Sunset Blvd, #601, Los Angeles 90069
F/V: features, commercials, documentaries, shorts. Bob Yamin, pres; Henri Bollinger, vp. (1968/4)

Turbine Films Int.   (212) 580-0532
140 W. 69th St., New York, NY 10023
F: features including Joey, TV commercials. Joe Ellison, prod/dir/writer.

The Turman-Foster Company   (213) 558-6906
10202 W. Washington Blvd, Culver City 90230
F: features including Mass Appeal and The Mean Season. Lawrence Turman; David Foster; Larry Foster, Mark Kruger. (1974)

Twentieth Century-Fox Film Corp.   (213) 277-2211
10201 West Pico Blvd, Los Angeles 90035
Mailing address: P O Box 900, Beverly Hills 90213
Barry Diller, chairman, CEO. Division include:

Twentieth Century-Fox Motion Pictures
F/V: features. Joe Wizan, president, film production.

Twentient-Century-Fox TV Harris Katlenan, pres; Leslie Moonves, vp TV movies and miniseries production.
TV series: Charlie & Company, Trappr John MD, Mr. Belvedere, Fall Guy.

u

UA (United Artists Corporation)   **(213) 202-0202**
10202 W. Washington Blvd, Culver City 90230
F: features. Division of MGM-UA Entertainment.

Ultra Film Service, Inc   **(213) 466-7972, 466-8809**
1159 N. Highland Ave. #B, Hollywood 90038
F: post production and sound transfer. Foley & ADR
stages. (1977/2)

Unger Productions   **(213) 553-5010**
2029 Century Pk. East #460, Los Angeles 90067
Motion picture and TV production company. Anthony
Unger, pres; Beverly Shurden, exec asst.

United TV Broadcasting System (UTB)   **(213) 467-4044**
6601 Hollywood Blvd, Hollywood 90028
F/V: TV series, commercials, B&I. Specializing in
productions in Japanese. Yasushi Haneda, exec prod.
(1970/20)

Universal City Studios   **(818) 985-4321**

100 Universal City Plaza, Universal City 91608
A division of MCA Inc. Lew Wasserman, Chairman, CEO
Divisons include:

Universal Pictures
F: features.

Universal Television
Robert Harris, pres.

TV series: Magnum P.I., Simon & Simon, Knight Rider,
Airwold, Alfred Hitchcock Presents, Amazing Stories,
George Burns Comedy Week, Miami Vice, Misfits of
Science, Murder She Wrote, The Equalizer, The In-
siders, Blacke's Magic, He's the Mayor.

Ed Masket, sen vp, administration; Kerry McCluggage,
sen vp, creative affairs; Earl Bellamy, sen vp,
production, Richard Lindheim, vp, series programing.
Craig Kellem, vp-comedy; Charmaine Ballain, vp-
drama; Peter Terranova vp-talent acquisition; Milt
Hammerman, vp-casting; Tom Thayer, vp-movies for TV;
Ben Halpern, vp-publicity.

U P A Productions of America   **(213) 556-3800**
1875 Century Park E #2140, Los Angeles 90067
Distribution of films, TV. Production of animated
and live action programs and commercials. Also licensing of characters. Henry G. Saperstein, pres.
Dorothy Schechter, vp; S. Richard Krown, vp;
Patricia Saperstein, marketing. (1950)

Tony Urbano Productions   **(213) 826-7214**
1322 Pacific Ave, Venice 90291
F/V: commercials, TV specials, series, B&I, features. Specialty is puppets, character costumes,
mechanical effects. (1964/5)

V

Renee Valente Productions   **(213) 203-2012**
Box 900, Beverly Hills 90213
F: independent company singed to 20th Century for TV
series but non-exclusive for features. Renee
Valente, pres; Burr Smidt, vp. (1977)

Valiant International Pictures, Inc   **(213) 665-5257**
4774 Melrose Ave, Hollywood 90029
F/V: features. And distributor. (1963/10) TLX:677408

VCE, Inc (Visual Concept Engineering) **(213) 463-9187**
1157 N. Highland Ave, Hollywood 90038
Special effects & animation for features including
Return of the Jedi. Peter Kuran, pres. (1978/10)

Velasco-Cardinale & Associates   **(213) 466-8556**
650 N. Bronson Ave #102, Hollywood 90004
Public relations/promotions (corporate & entertainment) including 1982-83 East LA Christmas Parade.
Jerry Velasco, Marcela Cardinale, Mike Gomez.

Viacom Productions, Inc   **(213) 208-2700**
10900 Wilshire Blvd 7th Fl,Los Angeles 90024
F/V: TV programs including Life and Times of Robert
Kennedy and Kids Don't Tell. Thomas Tannenbaum,
pres; Lloyd Weintraub, vp development.

Video-it, Inc   (213) 876-4055 (VIDEOIT)
1016 N. Sycamore Ave, Hollywood 90038
V: commercials, shorts. (1978/5)

Video Dimensions   (213) 417-8871 417-8279
5763 Uplander Way, Culver City 90230
V: complete production/post production faciltiy.
Dwight Blackshear, video consultant.

The Video Network, Inc   (213) 461-2534
1832 N. Gower St, Hollywood 90028
V: commercial, travel, music, newsreel; full post
production video services. Pete Bogner, CEO; Carl
Ofert, vp operations.

Vik-Winkle Productions, Inc   (818) 843-1920
729 N. Victory Blvd, Burbank 91502
F/V: commercials, B&I. Ed Winkle, pres; David Vik,
vp. (1970/6)

Vision II   (213) 385-6363, TLX: 19-4960
1543 W. Olympic Blvd #543. Los Angeles 90015
F/V: commercials in Spanish. A subsidiary of Vision
(Spanish) Advertising, Inc: nationwide producer of
Spanish AV materials. Luis Vargas, dir; Nel De
Vargas, vp; Carmen Hensch, media planning. Manuel
Barrancos, art director. (1974/7)

Fran von Zerneck Films   (818) 766-2610
4121 Radford Ave, Studio City 91604
F: features including Obsessive Love, Invitation to
Hell; and TV specials. Frank von Zerneck, exec prod;
Robert M. Sertner, prod; Barbara Bunning, develop-
ment. (1976/12)

W

Raymond Wagner Productions   (213) 203-1925
Mailing address: Box 900, Beverly Hills, 90213
F:features. (1968/3)

Brad Waisbren Enterprises (818) 506-3000
PO Box 8741, Universal City 91608
Development, packaging, and production of features,
TV, and videocassettes. Also supply name talent for
productions by other companies, includes commercials. Brad Waisbren, pres; Michael Palozzolo,vp
creative affairs; Beth Pickford mgr operations.

Kent Wakeford & Associates (213) 876-9971
3330 Barham Blvd, Los Angeles 90068
F/V: documentaries, commercials. Arthur Scarmeas,
exec producer. (1975/4)

Wallach Enterprises, Inc (213) 278-4574
1400 Braeridge Dr, Beverly Hills 90210
Management: sports & entertainment. George Wallach,
pres; Burt Shapiro, vp.

Chet Wallen Films (213) 963-2055
160 N. San Jose Dr, Glendora 91740
Library of auto racing films. Stock footage.
(1976/2)

Hal Wallis Productions 273-3381
9200 Sunset Blvd. #1201, Los Angeles 90069
F: features.

Warner Brothers, Inc (818) 954-6000
4000 Warner Blvd, Burbank 91522
F: features

Warner Bros. Television Programming (818) 954-6000
Alan Shayne, pres; Scott Seigler, sen vp, creative
affairs; development: Norman Stephens, vp-TV movies
and miniseries; Gary Credle, vp TV production; Davic
Sacks, vp-current programing; Larry Little, vp;
Cindy Dunne, vp.
Series: Night Court (Reinhold Weege, exec prod;
Jeffrey Melman, superv prod), Scarecrow and Mrs.
King (George Geiger, exec prod; Superv prod Rob
Gilmore), Growing Pains (Arnold Margolin, prod; Mike
Sullivan, exec prod; Neal Marlens co-prod), Shadow
Chasers (Ken Johnson, exec prod; Brian Glazer co-
exec prod), I Had Three Wives (John Wilder, exec
prod; Bill Yates, superv prod), Spenser for Hire
(Carla Singer, exec prod; Nick Thiel, co-exec prod;
Tom Chehak, superv prod).

Eric Weaver Productions　　　　**(213) 245-0308**
315 Harvey Dr, Glendale 91206
F/V: features and TV series. Eric Weaver, pres.

Fred Weintraub Productions　　　　**(213) 558-6428**
10202 Washington Blvd, Culver City 90230
F: features including Enter the Dragon, High Road to
China. Fred Weintraub, producer.

Jerry Weintraub　　　　**(818) 954-3754**
4000 Warner Blvd, Burbank 91523
F: TV and features including Diner. TV: David
Dworski; features: Gary Burkhart.

Barry Weitz Films, Inc　　　　**(818) 760-6125**
4024 Radford, Studio City 91604
F: features. Barry Weitz, pres.

West Entertainment, Inc　　　　**(213) 654-1096**
P O Box 46567, Hollywood 90046
F/V: commercials, TV, features. Also distribution.
Masaaki Asuka, pres; Fudge Yamashita, vp. (1971/3)

West Wind Productions　　　　**(818) 769-5900**
12206 Magnolia Blvd, North Hollywood 91607
F/V: commercials, documentaries, B&I. Jack Silver,
producer-dir. (1973/4)

Westlake Audio　　　　**(213) 654-2155, TLX: 698645**
8447 Beverly Blvd, Los Angeles 90048
Recording of music and spoken word for TV, movies,
commercials, and records. Judy Spreen, studio manager.(1978/20)

Wexler Film Productions　　　　**(213) 462-6671**
801 N. Seward St, Los Angeles 90038
F: health education and medical education. Sy
Wexler, pres. (1960/10)

Ruth White Films　　　　**(213) 836-4678**
P O Box 34485, Los Angeles 90034
F: education. Division of Rhythms Productions: rec-
ord and book publishing. (1956/4)

Thelma White Productions　　　　**(818) 894-3336**
8431 Lennox Ave., Panorama City 91402
F: features. (1969/3)

100

Whitefeather Productions, Inc.   (213) 937-3737
116 S. La Brea Ave, Los Angeles 90036
Packaging company bringing together film, TV, and
cable properties with financial, distribution, and
creative elements. Office in London. Bill Cameron,
pres; Robert Pilkington-Miksa, exec vp.

Whyaduck Productions, Inc   (213) 276-2324
9110 Sunset Blvd #120, Los Angeles 90069
Production and development of features for TV, primarily compilation documentary specials including
The Marx Brothers in a Nutshell. Robert Weide, pres,
prod.

Wildwood Enterprises   (818) 954-3221
4000 Warner Blvd, Burbank 91522
F: features including Ordinary People. Robert
Redford, producer-director.

Robert Wise Productions   (213) 461-3864
1438 N. Gower (#562), Hollywood 90028
F: features including Star Trek. Robert Wise, producer-director.

Witt/Thomas Productions   (213) 464-1333
1438 N Gower, Los Angeles 90028
F/V: TV series, features. Paul Junger Witt; Tony
Thomas.

Witt-Thomas-Harris Productions   (213) 464-1333
1438 N. Gower, Los Angeles 90028
F/V: TV series Benson, and features. Sue Palladino,
program development. Paul Junger Witt, Tony Thomas,
Susan Harris.

Witzend Productions   (213) 462-6185
1600 N. Highland Ave, Los Angeles 90028
F/V: TV series: situation comedies and pilots. Office in London. Allan McKeown, CEO; Ian LaFrenais,
writer-producer; Bryan Burch-Worch, dir creative
affairs. (1978/2)

WK Productions,   (213) 312-4803
11500 W. Olympic Blvd #300, Los Angeles 90064
See: William Kayden Productions

Robert Wold Company   **(213) 474-3500**
10880 Wilshire Blvd. #2204, Los Angeles 90024
V: Live and taped ad hoc network telecasts and
closed circuit live and taped video events. Religious and Israeli-oriented programs. Videoconfer-
ences. K.N. Wold, chairman; Gary Worth, pres; Robert
E. Wold, marketing. (1977/80). NY: (212) 832-3666
(1970/80)

David L. Wolper Productions, Inc.   **(818) 954-1707**
4000 Warner Blvd, Burbank 91522
F/V: TV programs, documentaries, features, mini-
series. David L. Wolper, pres-producer.

Woodholly Productions   **(213) 462-5330**
712 H.Seward St, Los Angeles 90038
Full recording services, magnetic transfers, video
services. Also camera rental (16mm 35mm and videotape). Post production facility with film editorial
service.

World Wide Pictures   **(818) 843-1300**
2520 W. Olive, Burbank 91505
F: religious films for churches and theatres.

Worldwide Productions   **(213) 273-7800**
3305 W. Spring Mountain Rd #60, Las Vegas NV 89102
dba Steve Krantz Productions
Motion picture/TV production. Steve Krantz, Judith
Krantz, Rhoda Lesh, Ann Muller.

Wrather Corporation   **(213) 278-8521**
270 N. Canon Dr, Beverly Hills 90210
Distributor of film series (including Lassie films)
through separately incorporated divisions. Owner of
Queen Mary, Spruce Goose, and other properties. Jack
Wrather, pres.

Y

Frank Yablans   **(213) 859-0461**
Northcorp Inc,
9200 Sunset Blvd #915, Los Angeles 90230
F: features including Monsignor.

Bud Yorkin Productions   (213) 202-3230
9336 W. Washington Blvd, Culver City 90230
F: producer of motion pictures. Bud Yorkin, pres;
William Hayes, business affairs.

Yorktown Productions   (213) 202-3402
9336 W. Washington Blvd, Culver City 90230
F: features including Best Friends, Iceman, A Sol-
dier's Story. Norman Jewison, dir-producer.

Z

The Zanuck/Brown Company   (213) 274-0261
202 N Canon Dr, Beverly Hills 90210
F: features including Cocoon. Richard Zanuck, pres;
David Brown, vp. (1972/9)

Zenith International Pictures Corp.   (213) 274-6033
1537 Benedict Canyon Dr, Beverly Hills 90210
F: features including Astral Factor. (1970/4)

Zephyr Productions   (818) 985-2940
11350 Ventura Blvd, Studio City 91604
F: features inlcuding Jimmy the Kid. Lawrence
Kuppin, Harry Evans Sloan, exec producers; Ronald
Jacobs, producer.

Zimmerman, Galanty, & Fiman   (213) 462-7353
1640 5th St. #202, Santa Monica 90401
M: tailored to liberal political and social con-
scious organizations. Mark Galanty, production mgr.
Also producers of home videos including the Jane
Fonda Workout Series.(1969/6)

Zimwar Productions   (213) 203-3394 203-1235
Box 900, Beverly Hills 90213
F: features. Vernon Zimmerman, Ronald Warranch

Zoetrope Studios   (415) 788-7500
916 Kearny St, San Francisco 94133
F: features including Rumble Fish. Francis Ford
Coppola, artistic dir.

INDEX

This index contains the names of personnel included in each company's listing. It also has other information regarding the companies. E.g. under the index heading "Music Video" is given all of the producers of music videos.

The numbers refer to pages of the directory.

The index does not include the names of the production company themselves as this book already lists them in alphabetical order.

Ross, D, 65
Ross, S, 68
Ross, M, 69
Ross, Jeff, 94
Roter, 79
Roven, 80
Roverato, 32
Rowe, 17
Royce, 32
Rubalcava, 73
Rubin, C, 25
Rubin, R, 48
Rubinich, 85
Rubinstein, 47
Ruby, 80
Ruddy, 80
Rushlow, 75
Rushton, 18

S
Sabinson, 84
Sack, 79
Sackett, 91
Sacks, 99
Safarik, 74
Sahl, 9
Salenger, 81
Sallan, 1
Salzburg, 81
Samples, 20
Samuelson, 49
Sanders, 88
Sandler, 66
Sanitsky, 93
Saparoff, 25
Saperstein, 97
Sargent, 70
Sawicki, 26
Saxton, 82
Scarecrow and Mrs. King, 99
Scarmeas, 99
Scenic drops, 36
Schaefer, 82
Schechter, 97
Scheer, 18
Scheimer, 34

Scheinfeld, 67
Schickler, 40
Schiller, 86
Schmidt, B, 3
Schmidt, M, 46
Schmit, 6
Schnitzer, 82
Schoenbrun, 72
Schoenburg, 78
Schroeder, 39
Schultz, 82
Schwab, 65
Schwartz, A, 21
Schwartz, J, 27
Schwartzberg, 31
Seaver, 84
Seidenglanz, 71
Seigler, 99
Seligman, 48
Seminars, 88
Sertner, 98
Seydor, 38
Shadow Chasers, 99
Shapiro, 99
Sharratt, 7
Shawley, 30
Shayne, 99
Sheets, 64
Sheldon, 51
Shirar, 48
Shoemaker, 84
Shurden, 96
Siegman, 85
Silver, A, 84,
Silver , P, 86
Silver, J, 100
Silver Spoons, 30
Silverman, 60
Simon, 85
Simon & Simon, 96
Simons, 22
Sims, 85
Singer, C, 18, 99
Singer, M, 47
Skaggs, 70
Skeeter, 17
Skolnek, 38

NOTE TO PRODUCERS

If you are now listed, please let us know as soon as possible about any changes and/or errors in your lisitng.

If you wish to be listed, please supply us with a clear and specific statent of what your company does and include at least the following information:

1) Name and address

2) The media in which you work.

3) The categories within which you work, e.g. features, TV series, commercials, business & industrial shorts, etc. If you work in a number of categories please use %. (e.g. 50% TV commercials, 40% B&I, 5% features, 5% music videos)

4) Other areas in which you work; or more specific statements about your work.

5) The year your company was founded.

6) The number of full time employees.

7) Names of key personnel and their positions (e.g. president, producer, production manager, vp-development, casting).

Send to: THE PRODUCERS
P. O. Box 1016
Venice, CA 90294-1016

Names and addresses of the listings in this directory are available on self-sticking address labels. For more information:

Richard Burger (213) 392-5165